The Personal Journal Of:

_____

_____

Year

Seat of Your Soul

Gratitude & Growth Journal

January 1

DAILY FOCUS: _____

DAILY COMMITMENT: _____
_____
_____

DAILY TOP TARGET: _____
_____
_____
_____

DAILY FOCUSED MEDITATION:

"I breathe in _____, I breathe out _____."

DAILY GOALS:	DAILY FOCUS:
_____	_____
_____	_____
_____	_____
_____	_____
_____	_____
_____	_____
_____	_____
_____	_____
_____	_____

NIGHTLY SUCCESS RECAP: _____
_____
_____
_____
_____
_____
_____

NIGHTLY GRATITUDE:_____
_____
_____
_____
_____
_____
_____

January 2

DAILY FOCUS: _____

DAILY COMMITMENT: _____
_____
_____

DAILY TOP TARGET: _____
_____
_____
_____

DAILY FOCUSED MEDITATION:

"I breathe in _____, I breathe out _____."

DAILY GOALS:	**DAILY FOCUS:**
_____	_____
_____	_____
_____	_____
_____	_____
_____	_____
_____	_____
_____	_____
_____	_____
_____	_____

NIGHTLY SUCCESS RECAP: _____
_____
_____
_____
_____
_____
_____

NIGHTLY GRATITUDE: _____
_____
_____
_____
_____
_____

January 3

DAILY FOCUS: _____

DAILY COMMITMENT: _____
_____
_____

DAILY TOP TARGET: _____
_____
_____
_____

DAILY FOCUSED MEDITATION:

"I breathe in _____, I breathe out _____."

DAILY GOALS: DAILY FOCUS:

_____   _____
_____   _____
_____   _____
_____   _____
_____   _____
_____   _____
_____   _____
_____   _____

NIGHTLY SUCCESS RECAP: _____
_____
_____
_____
_____
_____

NIGHTLY GRATITUDE:_____
_____
_____
_____
_____
_____

January 4

DAILY FOCUS: _____

DAILY COMMITMENT: _____
_____
_____

DAILY TOP TARGET: _____
_____
_____
_____

DAILY FOCUSED MEDITATION:

"I breathe in _____, I breathe out _____."

DAILY GOALS:	**DAILY FOCUS:**
_____	_____
_____	_____
_____	_____
_____	_____
_____	_____
_____	_____
_____	_____
_____	_____
_____	_____

NIGHTLY SUCCESS RECAP: _____
_____
_____
_____
_____
_____

NIGHTLY GRATITUDE: _____
_____
_____
_____
_____
_____

January 5

DAILY FOCUS: _____

DAILY COMMITMENT: _____
_____
_____

DAILY TOP TARGET: _____
_____
_____
_____

DAILY FOCUSED MEDITATION:

"I breathe in _____, I breathe out _____."

DAILY GOALS:	**DAILY FOCUS:**
_____	_____
_____	_____
_____	_____
_____	_____
_____	_____
_____	_____
_____	_____
_____	_____
_____	_____

NIGHTLY SUCCESS RECAP: _____
_____
_____
_____
_____
_____

NIGHTLY GRATITUDE:_____
_____
_____
_____
_____
_____
_____

January 6

DAILY FOCUS: _____

DAILY COMMITMENT: _____
_____
_____

DAILY TOP TARGET: _____
_____
_____
_____

DAILY FOCUSED MEDITATION:

"I breathe in _____, I breathe out _____."

DAILY GOALS:

_____
_____
_____
_____
_____
_____
_____
_____
_____

DAILY FOCUS:

_____
_____
_____
_____
_____
_____
_____
_____
_____

NIGHTLY SUCCESS RECAP: _____
_____
_____
_____
_____
_____

NIGHTLY GRATITUDE: _____
_____
_____
_____
_____
_____
_____

January 7

DAILY FOCUS: _____

DAILY COMMITMENT: _____
_____
_____

DAILY TOP TARGET: _____
_____
_____
_____

DAILY FOCUSED MEDITATION:

"I breathe in _____, I breathe out _____."

DAILY GOALS: DAILY FOCUS:

_____   _____
_____   _____
_____   _____
_____   _____
_____   _____
_____   _____
_____   _____
_____   _____

NIGHTLY SUCCESS RECAP: _____
_____
_____
_____
_____
_____

NIGHTLY GRATITUDE: _____
_____
_____
_____
_____
_____

January 8

DAILY FOCUS: _____

DAILY COMMITMENT: _____
_____
_____

DAILY TOP TARGET: _____
_____
_____
_____

DAILY FOCUSED MEDITATION:

"I breathe in _____, I breathe out _____."

DAILY GOALS: **DAILY FOCUS:**

_____   _____
_____   _____
_____   _____
_____   _____
_____   _____
_____   _____
_____   _____
_____   _____
_____   _____

NIGHTLY SUCCESS RECAP: _____
_____
_____
_____
_____
_____

NIGHTLY GRATITUDE: _____
_____
_____
_____
_____
_____

January 9

DAILY FOCUS: _____

DAILY COMMITMENT: _____
_____
_____

DAILY TOP TARGET: _____
_____
_____
_____

DAILY FOCUSED MEDITATION:

"I breathe in _____, I breathe out _____."

DAILY GOALS:

_____
_____
_____
_____
_____
_____
_____
_____
_____

DAILY FOCUS:

_____
_____
_____
_____
_____
_____
_____
_____
_____

NIGHTLY SUCCESS RECAP: _____
_____
_____
_____
_____
_____

NIGHTLY GRATITUDE: _____
_____
_____
_____
_____
_____

January 10

DAILY FOCUS: _____

DAILY COMMITMENT: _____
_____
_____

DAILY TOP TARGET: _____
_____
_____
_____

DAILY FOCUSED MEDITATION:

"I breathe in _____, I breathe out _____."

DAILY GOALS:

_____
_____
_____
_____
_____
_____
_____
_____
_____
_____

DAILY FOCUS:

_____
_____
_____
_____
_____
_____
_____
_____
_____
_____

NIGHTLY SUCCESS RECAP: _____
_____
_____
_____
_____
_____

NIGHTLY GRATITUDE: _____
_____
_____
_____
_____
_____

January 11

DAILY FOCUS: _____

DAILY COMMITMENT: _____
_____
_____

DAILY TOP TARGET: _____
_____
_____
_____

DAILY FOCUSED MEDITATION:

"I breathe in _____, I breathe out _____."

DAILY GOALS: DAILY FOCUS:

_____ _____
_____ _____
_____ _____
_____ _____
_____ _____
_____ _____
_____ _____
_____ _____
_____ _____

NIGHTLY SUCCESS RECAP: _____
_____
_____
_____
_____
_____
_____

NIGHTLY GRATITUDE: _____
_____
_____
_____
_____
_____
_____

January 12

DAILY FOCUS: _____

DAILY COMMITMENT: _____
_____
_____

DAILY TOP TARGET: _____
_____
_____
_____

DAILY FOCUSED MEDITATION:

"I breathe in _____, I breathe out _____."

DAILY GOALS:	**DAILY FOCUS:**
_____	_____
_____	_____
_____	_____
_____	_____
_____	_____
_____	_____
_____	_____
_____	_____
_____	_____

NIGHTLY SUCCESS RECAP: _____
_____
_____
_____
_____
_____

NIGHTLY GRATITUDE: _____
_____
_____
_____
_____
_____
_____

January 13

DAILY FOCUS: _____

DAILY COMMITMENT: _____
_____
_____

DAILY TOP TARGET: _____
_____
_____
_____

DAILY FOCUSED MEDITATION:

"I breathe in _____, I breathe out _____."

DAILY GOALS:	DAILY FOCUS:
_____	_____
_____	_____
_____	_____
_____	_____
_____	_____
_____	_____
_____	_____
_____	_____

NIGHTLY SUCCESS RECAP: _____
_____
_____
_____
_____
_____

NIGHTLY GRATITUDE: _____
_____
_____
_____
_____
_____

January 14

DAILY FOCUS: _____

DAILY COMMITMENT: _____
_____
_____

DAILY TOP TARGET: _____
_____
_____
_____

DAILY FOCUSED MEDITATION:

"I breathe in _____, I breathe out _____."

DAILY GOALS: **DAILY FOCUS:**

_____   _____
_____   _____
_____   _____
_____   _____
_____   _____
_____   _____
_____   _____
_____   _____
_____   _____
_____   _____

NIGHTLY SUCCESS RECAP: _____
_____
_____
_____
_____
_____
_____

NIGHTLY GRATITUDE: _____
_____
_____
_____
_____
_____
_____

January 15

DAILY FOCUS: _____

DAILY COMMITMENT: _____
_____
_____

DAILY TOP TARGET: _____
_____
_____
_____

DAILY FOCUSED MEDITATION:

"I breathe in _____, I breathe out _____."

DAILY GOALS: DAILY FOCUS:

_____   _____
_____   _____
_____   _____
_____   _____
_____   _____
_____   _____
_____   _____
_____   _____
_____   _____

NIGHTLY SUCCESS RECAP: _____
_____
_____
_____
_____
_____
_____

NIGHTLY GRATITUDE:_____
_____
_____
_____
_____
_____
_____

DAILY FOCUS: _____

DAILY COMMITMENT: _____
_____
_____

DAILY TOP TARGET: _____
_____
_____
_____

DAILY FOCUSED MEDITATION:

"I breathe in _____, I breathe out _____."

        DAILY GOALS: **DAILY FOCUS:**

_____   _____
_____   _____
_____   _____
_____   _____
_____   _____
_____   _____
_____   _____
_____   _____
_____   _____

NIGHTLY SUCCESS RECAP: _____
_____
_____
_____
_____
_____

NIGHTLY GRATITUDE:_____
_____
_____
_____
_____
_____
_____

January 17

DAILY FOCUS: _____

DAILY COMMITMENT: _____
_____
_____

DAILY TOP TARGET: _____
_____
_____
_____

DAILY FOCUSED MEDITATION:

"I breathe in _____, I breathe out _____."

DAILY GOALS:

_____
_____
_____
_____
_____
_____
_____
_____
_____

DAILY FOCUS:

_____
_____
_____
_____
_____
_____
_____
_____
_____

NIGHTLY SUCCESS RECAP: _____
_____
_____
_____
_____
_____
_____

NIGHTLY GRATITUDE: _____
_____
_____
_____
_____
_____
_____

January 18

DAILY FOCUS: _____

DAILY COMMITMENT: _____
_____
_____

DAILY TOP TARGET: _____
_____
_____
_____

DAILY FOCUSED MEDITATION:

"I breathe in _____, I breathe out _____."

DAILY GOALS:	**DAILY FOCUS:**
_____	_____
_____	_____
_____	_____
_____	_____
_____	_____
_____	_____
_____	_____
_____	_____
_____	_____

NIGHTLY SUCCESS RECAP: _____
_____
_____
_____
_____
_____
_____

NIGHTLY GRATITUDE: _____
_____
_____
_____
_____
_____
_____

January 19

DAILY FOCUS: _____

DAILY COMMITMENT: _____
_____
_____

DAILY TOP TARGET: _____
_____
_____
_____

DAILY FOCUSED MEDITATION:

"I breathe in _____, I breathe out _____."

DAILY GOALS: **DAILY FOCUS:**

_____   _____
_____   _____
_____   _____
_____   _____
_____   _____
_____   _____
_____   _____
_____   _____
_____   _____

NIGHTLY SUCCESS RECAP: _____
_____
_____
_____
_____
_____

NIGHTLY GRATITUDE: _____
_____
_____
_____
_____
_____
_____

January 20

DAILY FOCUS: _____

DAILY COMMITMENT: _____
_____
_____

DAILY TOP TARGET: _____
_____
_____
_____

DAILY FOCUSED MEDITATION:

"I breathe in _____, I breathe out _____."

DAILY GOALS: **DAILY FOCUS:**

_____   _____
_____   _____
_____   _____
_____   _____
_____   _____
_____   _____
_____   _____
_____   _____
_____   _____

NIGHTLY SUCCESS RECAP: _____
_____
_____
_____
_____
_____

NIGHTLY GRATITUDE: _____
_____
_____
_____
_____
_____

January 21

DAILY FOCUS: _____

DAILY COMMITMENT: _____
_____
_____

DAILY TOP TARGET: _____
_____
_____
_____

DAILY FOCUSED MEDITATION:

"I breathe in _____, I breathe out _____."

DAILY GOALS:

_____
_____
_____
_____
_____
_____
_____
_____

DAILY FOCUS:

_____
_____
_____
_____
_____
_____
_____
_____
_____

NIGHTLY SUCCESS RECAP: _____
_____
_____
_____
_____
_____

NIGHTLY GRATITUDE:_____
_____
_____
_____
_____
_____

January 22

DAILY FOCUS: _____

DAILY COMMITMENT: _____
_____
_____

DAILY TOP TARGET: _____
_____
_____
_____

DAILY FOCUSED MEDITATION:

"I breathe in _____, I breathe out _____."

DAILY GOALS: **DAILY FOCUS:**

_____   _____
_____   _____
_____   _____
_____   _____
_____   _____
_____   _____
_____   _____
_____   _____
_____   _____

NIGHTLY SUCCESS RECAP: _____
_____
_____
_____
_____
_____
_____

NIGHTLY GRATITUDE: _____
_____
_____
_____
_____
_____
_____

January 23

DAILY FOCUS: _____

DAILY COMMITMENT: _____
_____
_____

DAILY TOP TARGET: _____
_____
_____
_____

DAILY FOCUSED MEDITATION:

"I breathe in _____, I breathe out _____."

DAILY GOALS:	DAILY FOCUS:
_____	_____
_____	_____
_____	_____
_____	_____
_____	_____
_____	_____
_____	_____
_____	_____
_____	_____

NIGHTLY SUCCESS RECAP: _____
_____
_____
_____
_____
_____
_____

NIGHTLY GRATITUDE: _____
_____
_____
_____
_____
_____

January 24

DAILY FOCUS: _____

DAILY COMMITMENT: _____
_____
_____

DAILY TOP TARGET: _____
_____
_____
_____

DAILY FOCUSED MEDITATION:

"I breathe in _____, I breathe out _____."

DAILY GOALS: **DAILY FOCUS:**

_____   _____
_____   _____
_____   _____
_____   _____
_____   _____
_____   _____
_____   _____
_____   _____
_____   _____

NIGHTLY SUCCESS RECAP: _____
_____
_____
_____
_____
_____

NIGHTLY GRATITUDE: _____
_____
_____
_____
_____
_____
_____

January 25

DAILY FOCUS: _____

DAILY COMMITMENT: _____
_____
_____

DAILY TOP TARGET: _____
_____
_____
_____

DAILY FOCUSED MEDITATION:

"I breathe in _____, I breathe out _____."

DAILY GOALS:	DAILY FOCUS:
_____	_____
_____	_____
_____	_____
_____	_____
_____	_____
_____	_____
_____	_____
_____	_____
_____	_____

NIGHTLY SUCCESS RECAP: _____
_____
_____
_____
_____
_____
_____

NIGHTLY GRATITUDE: _____
_____
_____
_____
_____
_____
_____

January 26

DAILY FOCUS: _____

DAILY COMMITMENT: _____
_____
_____

DAILY TOP TARGET: _____
_____
_____
_____

DAILY FOCUSED MEDITATION:

"I breathe in _____, I breathe out _____."

DAILY GOALS:

_____
_____
_____
_____
_____
_____
_____
_____
_____
_____

DAILY FOCUS:

_____
_____
_____
_____
_____
_____
_____
_____
_____
_____

NIGHTLY SUCCESS RECAP: _____
_____
_____
_____
_____
_____
_____

NIGHTLY GRATITUDE: _____
_____
_____
_____
_____
_____
_____

January 27

DAILY FOCUS: _____

DAILY COMMITMENT: _____
_____
_____

DAILY TOP TARGET: _____
_____
_____
_____

DAILY FOCUSED MEDITATION:

"I breathe in _____, I breathe out _____."

DAILY GOALS:

_____
_____
_____
_____
_____
_____
_____
_____
_____

DAILY FOCUS:

_____
_____
_____
_____
_____
_____
_____
_____
_____

NIGHTLY SUCCESS RECAP: _____
_____
_____
_____
_____
_____
_____

NIGHTLY GRATITUDE: _____
_____
_____
_____
_____
_____
_____

January 28

DAILY FOCUS: _____

DAILY COMMITMENT: _____
_____
_____

DAILY TOP TARGET: _____
_____
_____
_____

DAILY FOCUSED MEDITATION:

"I breathe in _____, I breathe out _____."

DAILY GOALS:	**DAILY FOCUS:**
_____	_____
_____	_____
_____	_____
_____	_____
_____	_____
_____	_____
_____	_____
_____	_____
_____	_____

NIGHTLY SUCCESS RECAP: _____
_____
_____
_____
_____
_____

NIGHTLY GRATITUDE: _____
_____
_____
_____
_____
_____

January 29

DAILY FOCUS: _____

DAILY COMMITMENT: _____
_____
_____

DAILY TOP TARGET: _____
_____
_____
_____

DAILY FOCUSED MEDITATION:

"I breathe in _____, I breathe out _____."

DAILY GOALS:	**DAILY FOCUS:**
_____	_____
_____	_____
_____	_____
_____	_____
_____	_____
_____	_____
_____	_____
_____	_____
_____	_____

NIGHTLY SUCCESS RECAP: _____
_____
_____
_____
_____
_____
_____

NIGHTLY GRATITUDE:_____
_____
_____
_____
_____
_____
_____

January 30

DAILY FOCUS: _____

DAILY COMMITMENT: _____
_____
_____

DAILY TOP TARGET: _____
_____
_____
_____

DAILY FOCUSED MEDITATION:

"I breathe in _____, I breathe out _____."

DAILY GOALS:

_____
_____
_____
_____
_____
_____
_____
_____
_____

DAILY FOCUS:

_____
_____
_____
_____
_____
_____
_____
_____
_____

NIGHTLY SUCCESS RECAP: _____
_____
_____
_____
_____
_____

NIGHTLY GRATITUDE: _____
_____
_____
_____
_____
_____

January 31

DAILY FOCUS: _____

DAILY COMMITMENT: _____
_____
_____

DAILY TOP TARGET: _____
_____
_____
_____

DAILY FOCUSED MEDITATION:

"I breathe in _____, I breathe out _____."

DAILY GOALS:	**DAILY FOCUS:**
_____	_____
_____	_____
_____	_____
_____	_____
_____	_____
_____	_____
_____	_____
_____	_____

NIGHTLY SUCCESS RECAP: _____
_____
_____
_____
_____
_____
_____

NIGHTLY GRATITUDE: _____
_____
_____
_____
_____
_____
_____

DAILY FOCUS: _____

DAILY COMMITMENT: _____
_____
_____

DAILY TOP TARGET: _____
_____
_____
_____

DAILY FOCUSED MEDITATION:

"I breathe in _____, I breathe out _____."

DAILY GOALS:	**DAILY FOCUS:**
_____	_____
_____	_____
_____	_____
_____	_____
_____	_____
_____	_____
_____	_____
_____	_____
_____	_____

NIGHTLY SUCCESS RECAP: _____
_____
_____
_____
_____
_____
_____

NIGHTLY GRATITUDE:_____
_____
_____
_____
_____
_____
_____

February 2

DAILY FOCUS: _____

DAILY COMMITMENT: _____
_____
_____

DAILY TOP TARGET: _____
_____
_____
_____

DAILY FOCUSED MEDITATION:

"I breathe in _____, I breathe out _____."

DAILY GOALS:	**DAILY FOCUS:**
_____	_____
_____	_____
_____	_____
_____	_____
_____	_____
_____	_____
_____	_____
_____	_____
_____	_____

NIGHTLY SUCCESS RECAP: _____
_____
_____
_____
_____
_____

NIGHTLY GRATITUDE:_____
_____
_____
_____
_____
_____
_____

February 3

DAILY FOCUS: _____

DAILY COMMITMENT: _____
_____
_____

DAILY TOP TARGET: _____
_____
_____
_____

DAILY FOCUSED MEDITATION:

"I breathe in _____, I breathe out _____."

DAILY GOALS:	**DAILY FOCUS:**
_____	_____
_____	_____
_____	_____
_____	_____
_____	_____
_____	_____
_____	_____
_____	_____
_____	_____
_____	_____

NIGHTLY SUCCESS RECAP: _____
_____
_____
_____
_____
_____
_____

NIGHTLY GRATITUDE: _____
_____
_____
_____
_____
_____
_____

February 4

DAILY FOCUS: _____

DAILY COMMITMENT: _____
_____
_____

DAILY TOP TARGET: _____
_____
_____
_____

DAILY FOCUSED MEDITATION:

"I breathe in _____, I breathe out _____."

DAILY GOALS:	DAILY FOCUS:
_____	_____
_____	_____
_____	_____
_____	_____
_____	_____
_____	_____
_____	_____
_____	_____
_____	_____
_____	_____

NIGHTLY SUCCESS RECAP: _____
_____
_____
_____
_____
_____

NIGHTLY GRATITUDE:_____
_____
_____
_____
_____
_____
_____

DAILY FOCUS: _____

DAILY COMMITMENT: _____
_____
_____

DAILY TOP TARGET: _____
_____
_____
_____

DAILY FOCUSED MEDITATION:

"I breathe in _____, I breathe out _____."

DAILY GOALS:	**DAILY FOCUS:**
_____	_____
_____	_____
_____	_____
_____	_____
_____	_____
_____	_____
_____	_____
_____	_____
_____	_____
_____	_____

NIGHTLY SUCCESS RECAP: _____
_____
_____
_____
_____
_____
_____

NIGHTLY GRATITUDE:_____
_____
_____
_____
_____
_____
_____

February 6

DAILY FOCUS: _____

DAILY COMMITMENT: _____
_____
_____

DAILY TOP TARGET: _____
_____
_____
_____

DAILY FOCUSED MEDITATION:

"I breathe in _____, I breathe out _____."

DAILY GOALS: DAILY FOCUS:

_____   _____
_____   _____
_____   _____
_____   _____
_____   _____
_____   _____
_____   _____
_____   _____

NIGHTLY SUCCESS RECAP: _____
_____
_____
_____
_____
_____
_____

NIGHTLY GRATITUDE:_____
_____
_____
_____
_____
_____
_____

February 7

DAILY FOCUS: _____

DAILY COMMITMENT: _____
_____
_____

DAILY TOP TARGET: _____
_____
_____
_____

DAILY FOCUSED MEDITATION:

"I breathe in _____, I breathe out _____."

DAILY GOALS: **DAILY FOCUS:**

_____   _____
_____   _____
_____   _____
_____   _____
_____   _____
_____   _____
_____   _____
_____   _____
_____   _____
_____   _____

NIGHTLY SUCCESS RECAP: _____
_____
_____
_____
_____
_____
_____

NIGHTLY GRATITUDE: _____
_____
_____
_____
_____
_____
_____

February 8

DAILY FOCUS: _____

DAILY COMMITMENT: _____
_____
_____

DAILY TOP TARGET: _____
_____
_____
_____

DAILY FOCUSED MEDITATION:

"I breathe in _____, I breathe out _____."

DAILY GOALS:

_____
_____
_____
_____
_____
_____
_____
_____
_____

DAILY FOCUS:

_____
_____
_____
_____
_____
_____
_____
_____
_____

NIGHTLY SUCCESS RECAP: _____
_____
_____
_____
_____
_____
_____

NIGHTLY GRATITUDE: _____
_____
_____
_____
_____
_____
_____

February 9

DAILY FOCUS: _____

DAILY COMMITMENT: _____
_____
_____

DAILY TOP TARGET: _____
_____
_____
_____

DAILY FOCUSED MEDITATION:

"I breathe in _____, I breathe out _____."

DAILY GOALS: **DAILY FOCUS:**

_____   _____
_____   _____
_____   _____
_____   _____
_____   _____
_____   _____
_____   _____
_____   _____
_____   _____

NIGHTLY SUCCESS RECAP: _____
_____
_____
_____
_____
_____
_____

NIGHTLY GRATITUDE:_____
_____
_____
_____
_____
_____
_____

February 10

DAILY FOCUS: _____

DAILY COMMITMENT: _____
_____
_____

DAILY TOP TARGET: _____
_____
_____
_____

DAILY FOCUSED MEDITATION:

"I breathe in _____, I breathe out _____."

DAILY GOALS: DAILY FOCUS:

_____   _____
_____   _____
_____   _____
_____   _____
_____   _____
_____   _____
_____   _____
_____   _____
_____   _____

NIGHTLY SUCCESS RECAP: _____
_____
_____
_____
_____
_____
_____

NIGHTLY GRATITUDE:_____
_____
_____
_____
_____
_____
_____
_____

DAILY FOCUS: _____

DAILY COMMITMENT: _____
_____
_____

DAILY TOP TARGET: _____
_____
_____
_____

DAILY FOCUSED MEDITATION:

"I breathe in _____, I breathe out _____."

DAILY GOALS:	**DAILY FOCUS:**
_____	_____
_____	_____
_____	_____
_____	_____
_____	_____
_____	_____
_____	_____
_____	_____
_____	_____
_____	_____

NIGHTLY SUCCESS RECAP: _____
_____
_____
_____
_____
_____

NIGHTLY GRATITUDE: _____
_____
_____
_____
_____
_____
_____

February 12

DAILY FOCUS: _____

DAILY COMMITMENT: _____
_____
_____

DAILY TOP TARGET: _____
_____
_____
_____

DAILY FOCUSED MEDITATION:

"I breathe in _____, I breathe out _____."

DAILY GOALS: DAILY FOCUS:

_____   _____
_____   _____
_____   _____
_____   _____
_____   _____
_____   _____
_____   _____
_____   _____
_____   _____

NIGHTLY SUCCESS RECAP: _____
_____
_____
_____
_____
_____
_____

NIGHTLY GRATITUDE: _____
_____
_____
_____
_____
_____
_____

February 13

DAILY FOCUS: _____

DAILY COMMITMENT: _____
_____
_____

DAILY TOP TARGET: _____
_____
_____
_____

DAILY FOCUSED MEDITATION:

"I breathe in _____, I breathe out _____."

<table>
<tr><td align="center">DAILY GOALS:</td><td align="center">DAILY FOCUS:</td></tr>
</table>

NIGHTLY SUCCESS RECAP: _____
_____
_____
_____
_____
_____
_____

NIGHTLY GRATITUDE: _____
_____
_____
_____
_____
_____

February 14

DAILY FOCUS: _____

DAILY COMMITMENT: _____
_____
_____

DAILY TOP TARGET: _____
_____
_____
_____

DAILY FOCUSED MEDITATION:

"I breathe in _____, I breathe out _____."

DAILY GOALS:	**DAILY FOCUS:**
_____	_____
_____	_____
_____	_____
_____	_____
_____	_____
_____	_____
_____	_____
_____	_____

NIGHTLY SUCCESS RECAP: _____
_____
_____
_____
_____
_____
_____

NIGHTLY GRATITUDE: _____
_____
_____
_____
_____
_____
_____

February 15

DAILY FOCUS: _____

DAILY COMMITMENT: _____
_____
_____

DAILY TOP TARGET: _____
_____
_____
_____

DAILY FOCUSED MEDITATION:

"I breathe in _____, I breathe out _____."

DAILY GOALS: **DAILY FOCUS:**

_____   _____
_____   _____
_____   _____
_____   _____
_____   _____
_____   _____
_____   _____
_____   _____
_____   _____

NIGHTLY SUCCESS RECAP: _____
_____
_____
_____
_____
_____
_____

NIGHTLY GRATITUDE:_____
_____
_____
_____
_____
_____
_____

February 16

DAILY FOCUS: _____

DAILY COMMITMENT: _____
_____
_____

DAILY TOP TARGET: _____
_____
_____
_____

DAILY FOCUSED MEDITATION:

"I breathe in _____, I breathe out _____."

<table>
<tr><td align="center">**DAILY GOALS:**</td><td align="center">**DAILY FOCUS:**</td></tr>
</table>

DAILY GOALS:	DAILY FOCUS:
_____	_____
_____	_____
_____	_____
_____	_____
_____	_____
_____	_____
_____	_____
_____	_____
_____	_____
_____	_____

NIGHTLY SUCCESS RECAP: _____
_____
_____
_____
_____
_____

NIGHTLY GRATITUDE: _____
_____
_____
_____
_____
_____

February 17

DAILY FOCUS: _____

DAILY COMMITMENT: _____
_____
_____

DAILY TOP TARGET: _____
_____
_____

DAILY FOCUSED MEDITATION:

"I breathe in _____, I breathe out _____."

DAILY GOALS:	**DAILY FOCUS:**
_____	_____
_____	_____
_____	_____
_____	_____
_____	_____
_____	_____
_____	_____
_____	_____
_____	_____

NIGHTLY SUCCESS RECAP: _____
_____
_____
_____
_____
_____
_____

NIGHTLY GRATITUDE: _____
_____
_____
_____
_____
_____
_____

February 18

DAILY FOCUS: _____

DAILY COMMITMENT: _____
_____
_____

DAILY TOP TARGET: _____
_____
_____
_____

DAILY FOCUSED MEDITATION:

"I breathe in _____, I breathe out _____."

DAILY GOALS:

_____
_____
_____
_____
_____
_____
_____
_____
_____

DAILY FOCUS:

_____
_____
_____
_____
_____
_____
_____
_____
_____

NIGHTLY SUCCESS RECAP: _____
_____
_____
_____
_____
_____

NIGHTLY GRATITUDE: _____
_____
_____
_____
_____
_____
_____

DAILY FOCUS: _____

DAILY COMMITMENT: _____
_____
_____

DAILY TOP TARGET: _____
_____
_____
_____

DAILY FOCUSED MEDITATION:

"I breathe in _____, I breathe out _____."

DAILY GOALS: **DAILY FOCUS:**

_____   _____
_____   _____
_____   _____
_____   _____
_____   _____
_____   _____
_____   _____
_____   _____
_____   _____

NIGHTLY SUCCESS RECAP: _____
_____
_____
_____
_____
_____
_____

NIGHTLY GRATITUDE: _____
_____
_____
_____
_____
_____
_____

February 20

DAILY FOCUS: _____

DAILY COMMITMENT: _____
_____
_____

DAILY TOP TARGET: _____
_____
_____
_____

DAILY FOCUSED MEDITATION:

"I breathe in _____, I breathe out _____."

DAILY GOALS:	**DAILY FOCUS:**
_____	_____
_____	_____
_____	_____
_____	_____
_____	_____
_____	_____
_____	_____
_____	_____

NIGHTLY SUCCESS RECAP: _____
_____
_____
_____
_____
_____

NIGHTLY GRATITUDE: _____
_____
_____
_____
_____
_____

February 21

DAILY FOCUS: _____

DAILY COMMITMENT: _____
_____
_____

DAILY TOP TARGET: _____
_____
_____
_____

DAILY FOCUSED MEDITATION:

"I breathe in _____, I breathe out _____."

DAILY GOALS:	**DAILY FOCUS:**
_____	_____
_____	_____
_____	_____
_____	_____
_____	_____
_____	_____
_____	_____
_____	_____
_____	_____

NIGHTLY SUCCESS RECAP: _____
_____
_____
_____
_____
_____
_____

NIGHTLY GRATITUDE: _____
_____
_____
_____
_____
_____
_____

February 22

DAILY FOCUS: _____

DAILY COMMITMENT: _____
_____
_____

DAILY TOP TARGET: _____
_____
_____
_____

DAILY FOCUSED MEDITATION:

"I breathe in _____, I breathe out _____."

DAILY GOALS:	**DAILY FOCUS:**
_____	_____
_____	_____
_____	_____
_____	_____
_____	_____
_____	_____
_____	_____
_____	_____
_____	_____

NIGHTLY SUCCESS RECAP: _____
_____
_____
_____
_____
_____

NIGHTLY GRATITUDE:_____
_____
_____
_____
_____
_____

DAILY FOCUS: _____

DAILY COMMITMENT: _____
_____
_____

DAILY TOP TARGET: _____
_____
_____
_____

DAILY FOCUSED MEDITATION:

"I breathe in _____, I breathe out _____."

DAILY GOALS:	**DAILY FOCUS:**
_____	_____
_____	_____
_____	_____
_____	_____
_____	_____
_____	_____
_____	_____
_____	_____
_____	_____

NIGHTLY SUCCESS RECAP: _____
_____
_____
_____
_____
_____

NIGHTLY GRATITUDE:_____
_____
_____
_____
_____
_____

February 24

DAILY FOCUS: _____

DAILY COMMITMENT: _____
_____
_____

DAILY TOP TARGET: _____
_____
_____
_____

DAILY FOCUSED MEDITATION:

"I breathe in _____, I breathe out _____."

DAILY GOALS:	DAILY FOCUS:
_____	_____
_____	_____
_____	_____
_____	_____
_____	_____
_____	_____
_____	_____
_____	_____
_____	_____

NIGHTLY SUCCESS RECAP: _____
_____
_____
_____
_____
_____

NIGHTLY GRATITUDE:_____
_____
_____
_____
_____
_____
_____

DAILY FOCUS: _____

DAILY COMMITMENT: _____
_____
_____

DAILY TOP TARGET: _____
_____
_____
_____

DAILY FOCUSED MEDITATION:

"I breathe in _____, I breathe out _____."

DAILY GOALS:	**DAILY FOCUS:**
_____	_____
_____	_____
_____	_____
_____	_____
_____	_____
_____	_____
_____	_____
_____	_____

NIGHTLY SUCCESS RECAP: _____
_____
_____
_____
_____
_____
_____

NIGHTLY GRATITUDE: _____
_____
_____
_____
_____
_____
_____

February 26

DAILY FOCUS: _____

DAILY COMMITMENT: _____
_____
_____

DAILY TOP TARGET: _____
_____
_____
_____

DAILY FOCUSED MEDITATION:

"I breathe in _____, I breathe out _____."

DAILY GOALS:	DAILY FOCUS:
_____	_____
_____	_____
_____	_____
_____	_____
_____	_____
_____	_____
_____	_____
_____	_____

NIGHTLY SUCCESS RECAP: _____
_____
_____
_____
_____
_____
_____

NIGHTLY GRATITUDE: _____
_____
_____
_____
_____
_____
_____

February 27

DAILY FOCUS: _____

DAILY COMMITMENT: _____
_____
_____

DAILY TOP TARGET: _____
_____
_____
_____

DAILY FOCUSED MEDITATION:

"I breathe in _____, I breathe out _____."

DAILY GOALS:	DAILY FOCUS:
_____	_____
_____	_____
_____	_____
_____	_____
_____	_____
_____	_____
_____	_____
_____	_____
_____	_____

NIGHTLY SUCCESS RECAP: _____
_____
_____
_____
_____
_____

NIGHTLY GRATITUDE: _____
_____
_____
_____
_____
_____

February 28

DAILY FOCUS: _____

DAILY COMMITMENT: _____
_____
_____

DAILY TOP TARGET: _____
_____
_____
_____

DAILY FOCUSED MEDITATION:

"I breathe in _____, I breathe out _____."

DAILY GOALS:	**DAILY FOCUS:**
_____	_____
_____	_____
_____	_____
_____	_____
_____	_____
_____	_____
_____	_____
_____	_____
_____	_____

NIGHTLY SUCCESS RECAP: _____
_____
_____
_____
_____
_____
_____

NIGHTLY GRATITUDE: _____
_____
_____
_____
_____
_____
_____

February 29

DAILY FOCUS: _____

DAILY COMMITMENT: _____
_____
_____

DAILY TOP TARGET: _____
_____
_____
_____

DAILY FOCUSED MEDITATION:

"I breathe in _____, I breathe out _____."

DAILY GOALS: **DAILY FOCUS:**

_____   _____
_____   _____
_____   _____
_____   _____
_____   _____
_____   _____
_____   _____
_____   _____
_____   _____
_____   _____

NIGHTLY SUCCESS RECAP: _____
_____
_____
_____
_____
_____
_____

NIGHTLY GRATITUDE: _____
_____
_____
_____
_____
_____
_____

March 1

DAILY FOCUS: _____

DAILY COMMITMENT: _____
_____
_____

DAILY TOP TARGET: _____
_____
_____
_____

DAILY FOCUSED MEDITATION:

"I breathe in _____, I breathe out _____."

DAILY GOALS:	**DAILY FOCUS:**
_____	_____
_____	_____
_____	_____
_____	_____
_____	_____
_____	_____
_____	_____
_____	_____
_____	_____

NIGHTLY SUCCESS RECAP: _____
_____
_____
_____
_____
_____
_____

NIGHTLY GRATITUDE: _____
_____
_____
_____
_____
_____
_____

March 2

DAILY FOCUS: _____

DAILY COMMITMENT: _____
_____
_____

DAILY TOP TARGET: _____
_____
_____
_____

DAILY FOCUSED MEDITATION:

"I breathe in _____, I breathe out _____."

DAILY GOALS:	**DAILY FOCUS:**
_____	_____
_____	_____
_____	_____
_____	_____
_____	_____
_____	_____
_____	_____
_____	_____
_____	_____

NIGHTLY SUCCESS RECAP: _____
_____
_____
_____
_____
_____
_____

NIGHTLY GRATITUDE: _____
_____
_____
_____
_____
_____
_____

March 3

DAILY FOCUS: _____

DAILY COMMITMENT: _____
_____
_____

DAILY TOP TARGET: _____
_____
_____
_____

DAILY FOCUSED MEDITATION:

"I breathe in _____, I breathe out _____."

DAILY GOALS:

_____
_____
_____
_____
_____
_____
_____
_____
_____

DAILY FOCUS:

_____
_____
_____
_____
_____
_____
_____
_____
_____

NIGHTLY SUCCESS RECAP: _____
_____
_____
_____
_____
_____
_____

NIGHTLY GRATITUDE: _____
_____
_____
_____
_____
_____
_____

DAILY FOCUS: _____

DAILY COMMITMENT: _____
_____
_____

DAILY TOP TARGET: _____
_____
_____
_____

DAILY FOCUSED MEDITATION:

"I breathe in _____, I breathe out _____."

DAILY GOALS:	**DAILY FOCUS:**
_____	_____
_____	_____
_____	_____
_____	_____
_____	_____
_____	_____
_____	_____
_____	_____
_____	_____

NIGHTLY SUCCESS RECAP: _____
_____
_____
_____
_____
_____

NIGHTLY GRATITUDE: _____
_____
_____
_____
_____
_____

March 5

DAILY FOCUS: _____

DAILY COMMITMENT: _____
_____
_____

DAILY TOP TARGET: _____
_____
_____
_____

DAILY FOCUSED MEDITATION:

"I breathe in _____, I breathe out _____."

DAILY GOALS:	**DAILY FOCUS:**
_____	_____
_____	_____
_____	_____
_____	_____
_____	_____
_____	_____
_____	_____
_____	_____
_____	_____

NIGHTLY SUCCESS RECAP: _____
_____
_____
_____
_____
_____

NIGHTLY GRATITUDE: _____
_____
_____
_____
_____
_____

March 6

DAILY FOCUS: _____

DAILY COMMITMENT: _____
_____
_____

DAILY TOP TARGET: _____
_____
_____
_____

DAILY FOCUSED MEDITATION:

"I breathe in _____, I breathe out _____."

DAILY GOALS:	**DAILY FOCUS:**
_____	_____
_____	_____
_____	_____
_____	_____
_____	_____
_____	_____
_____	_____
_____	_____
_____	_____

NIGHTLY SUCCESS RECAP: _____
_____
_____
_____
_____
_____
_____

NIGHTLY GRATITUDE: _____
_____
_____
_____
_____
_____

March 7

DAILY FOCUS: _____

DAILY COMMITMENT: _____
_____
_____

DAILY TOP TARGET: _____
_____
_____
_____

DAILY FOCUSED MEDITATION:

"I breathe in _____, I breathe out _____."

DAILY GOALS:	DAILY FOCUS:
_____	_____
_____	_____
_____	_____
_____	_____
_____	_____
_____	_____
_____	_____
_____	_____
_____	_____

NIGHTLY SUCCESS RECAP: _____
_____
_____
_____
_____
_____
_____

NIGHTLY GRATITUDE:_____
_____
_____
_____
_____
_____
_____

DAILY FOCUS: _____

DAILY COMMITMENT: _____
_____
_____

DAILY TOP TARGET: _____
_____
_____
_____

DAILY FOCUSED MEDITATION:

"I breathe in _____, I breathe out _____."

DAILY GOALS:	**DAILY FOCUS:**
_____	_____
_____	_____
_____	_____
_____	_____
_____	_____
_____	_____
_____	_____
_____	_____
_____	_____
_____	_____

NIGHTLY SUCCESS RECAP: _____
_____
_____
_____
_____
_____

NIGHTLY GRATITUDE: _____
_____
_____
_____
_____
_____

March 9

DAILY FOCUS: _____

DAILY COMMITMENT: _____
_____
_____

DAILY TOP TARGET: _____
_____
_____
_____

DAILY FOCUSED MEDITATION:

"I breathe in _____, I breathe out _____."

DAILY GOALS:

_____
_____
_____
_____
_____
_____
_____
_____
_____

DAILY FOCUS:

_____
_____
_____
_____
_____
_____
_____
_____
_____

NIGHTLY SUCCESS RECAP: _____
_____
_____
_____
_____
_____
_____

NIGHTLY GRATITUDE:_____
_____
_____
_____
_____
_____
_____

DAILY FOCUS: _____

DAILY COMMITMENT: _____
_____
_____

DAILY TOP TARGET: _____
_____
_____
_____

DAILY FOCUSED MEDITATION:

"I breathe in _____, I breathe out _____."

DAILY GOALS: **DAILY FOCUS:**

_____   _____
_____   _____
_____   _____
_____   _____
_____   _____
_____   _____
_____   _____
_____   _____
_____   _____

NIGHTLY SUCCESS RECAP: _____
_____
_____
_____
_____
_____
_____

NIGHTLY GRATITUDE: _____
_____
_____
_____
_____
_____
_____

March 11

DAILY FOCUS: _____

DAILY COMMITMENT: _____
_____
_____

DAILY TOP TARGET: _____
_____
_____
_____

DAILY FOCUSED MEDITATION:

"I breathe in _____, I breathe out _____."

DAILY GOALS: DAILY FOCUS:

_____   _____
_____   _____
_____   _____
_____   _____
_____   _____
_____   _____
_____   _____
_____   _____
_____   _____
_____   _____

NIGHTLY SUCCESS RECAP: _____
_____
_____
_____
_____
_____
_____

NIGHTLY GRATITUDE: _____
_____
_____
_____
_____
_____
_____

March 12

DAILY FOCUS: _____

DAILY COMMITMENT: _____
_____
_____

DAILY TOP TARGET: _____
_____
_____
_____

DAILY FOCUSED MEDITATION:

"I breathe in _____, I breathe out _____."

DAILY GOALS:	DAILY FOCUS:
_____	_____
_____	_____
_____	_____
_____	_____
_____	_____
_____	_____
_____	_____
_____	_____
_____	_____

NIGHTLY SUCCESS RECAP: _____
_____
_____
_____
_____
_____

NIGHTLY GRATITUDE: _____
_____
_____
_____
_____
_____
_____

March 13

DAILY FOCUS: _____

DAILY COMMITMENT: _____
_____
_____

DAILY TOP TARGET: _____
_____
_____
_____

DAILY FOCUSED MEDITATION:

"I breathe in _____, I breathe out _____."

DAILY GOALS:	DAILY FOCUS:
_____	_____
_____	_____
_____	_____
_____	_____
_____	_____
_____	_____
_____	_____
_____	_____
_____	_____

NIGHTLY SUCCESS RECAP: _____
_____
_____
_____
_____
_____

NIGHTLY GRATITUDE:_____
_____
_____
_____
_____
_____
_____

March 14

DAILY FOCUS: _____

DAILY COMMITMENT: _____
_____
_____

DAILY TOP TARGET: _____
_____
_____
_____

DAILY FOCUSED MEDITATION:

"I breathe in _____, I breathe out _____."

DAILY GOALS:	**DAILY FOCUS:**
_____	_____
_____	_____
_____	_____
_____	_____
_____	_____
_____	_____
_____	_____
_____	_____
_____	_____

NIGHTLY SUCCESS RECAP: _____
_____
_____
_____
_____
_____

NIGHTLY GRATITUDE:_____
_____
_____
_____
_____
_____
_____

March 15

DAILY FOCUS: _____

DAILY COMMITMENT: _____
_____
_____

DAILY TOP TARGET: _____
_____
_____
_____

DAILY FOCUSED MEDITATION:

"I breathe in _____, I breathe out _____."

DAILY GOALS:	**DAILY FOCUS:**
_____	_____
_____	_____
_____	_____
_____	_____
_____	_____
_____	_____
_____	_____
_____	_____
_____	_____

NIGHTLY SUCCESS RECAP: _____
_____
_____
_____
_____
_____

NIGHTLY GRATITUDE: _____
_____
_____
_____
_____
_____

March 16

DAILY FOCUS: _____

DAILY COMMITMENT: _____
_____
_____

DAILY TOP TARGET: _____
_____
_____
_____

DAILY FOCUSED MEDITATION:

"I breathe in _____, I breathe out _____."

DAILY GOALS:	**DAILY FOCUS:**
_____	_____
_____	_____
_____	_____
_____	_____
_____	_____
_____	_____
_____	_____
_____	_____
_____	_____
_____	_____

NIGHTLY SUCCESS RECAP: _____
_____
_____
_____
_____
_____

NIGHTLY GRATITUDE: _____
_____
_____
_____
_____
_____
_____

March 17

DAILY FOCUS: _____

DAILY COMMITMENT: _____
_____
_____

DAILY TOP TARGET: _____
_____
_____
_____

DAILY FOCUSED MEDITATION:

"I breathe in _____, I breathe out _____."

DAILY GOALS:	DAILY FOCUS:
_____	_____
_____	_____
_____	_____
_____	_____
_____	_____
_____	_____
_____	_____
_____	_____
_____	_____

NIGHTLY SUCCESS RECAP: _____
_____
_____
_____
_____
_____
_____

NIGHTLY GRATITUDE: _____
_____
_____
_____
_____
_____
_____

DAILY FOCUS: _____

DAILY COMMITMENT: _____
_____
_____

DAILY TOP TARGET: _____
_____
_____
_____

DAILY FOCUSED MEDITATION:

"I breathe in _____, I breathe out _____."

DAILY GOALS:	**DAILY FOCUS:**
_____	_____
_____	_____
_____	_____
_____	_____
_____	_____
_____	_____
_____	_____
_____	_____
_____	_____

NIGHTLY SUCCESS RECAP: _____
_____
_____
_____
_____
_____
_____

NIGHTLY GRATITUDE: _____
_____
_____
_____
_____
_____
_____

March 19

DAILY FOCUS: _____

DAILY COMMITMENT: _____
_____
_____

DAILY TOP TARGET: _____
_____
_____
_____

DAILY FOCUSED MEDITATION:

"I breathe in _____, I breathe out _____."

DAILY GOALS: ### DAILY FOCUS:

_____   _____
_____   _____
_____   _____
_____   _____
_____   _____
_____   _____
_____   _____
_____   _____
_____   _____

NIGHTLY SUCCESS RECAP: _____
_____
_____
_____
_____
_____

NIGHTLY GRATITUDE:_____
_____
_____
_____
_____
_____
_____

DAILY FOCUS: _____

DAILY COMMITMENT: _____
_____
_____

DAILY TOP TARGET: _____
_____
_____
_____

DAILY FOCUSED MEDITATION:

"I breathe in _____, I breathe out _____."

DAILY GOALS: **DAILY FOCUS:**

_____   _____
_____   _____
_____   _____
_____   _____
_____   _____
_____   _____
_____   _____
_____   _____
_____   _____

NIGHTLY SUCCESS RECAP: _____
_____
_____
_____
_____
_____
_____

NIGHTLY GRATITUDE: _____
_____
_____
_____
_____
_____
_____

March 21

DAILY FOCUS: _____

DAILY COMMITMENT: _____
_____
_____

DAILY TOP TARGET: _____
_____
_____
_____

DAILY FOCUSED MEDITATION:

"I breathe in _____, I breathe out _____."

DAILY GOALS:	**DAILY FOCUS:**
_____	_____
_____	_____
_____	_____
_____	_____
_____	_____
_____	_____
_____	_____
_____	_____
_____	_____

NIGHTLY SUCCESS RECAP: _____
_____
_____
_____
_____
_____
_____

NIGHTLY GRATITUDE:_____
_____
_____
_____
_____
_____
_____

DAILY FOCUS: _____

DAILY COMMITMENT: _____
_____
_____

DAILY TOP TARGET: _____
_____
_____
_____

DAILY FOCUSED MEDITATION:

"I breathe in _____, I breathe out _____."

DAILY GOALS:	**DAILY FOCUS:**
_____	_____
_____	_____
_____	_____
_____	_____
_____	_____
_____	_____
_____	_____
_____	_____
_____	_____

NIGHTLY SUCCESS RECAP: _____
_____
_____
_____
_____
_____
_____

NIGHTLY GRATITUDE: _____
_____
_____
_____
_____
_____
_____

March 23

DAILY FOCUS: _____

DAILY COMMITMENT: _____
_____
_____

DAILY TOP TARGET: _____
_____
_____
_____

DAILY FOCUSED MEDITATION:

"I breathe in _____, I breathe out _____."

DAILY GOALS:

_____
_____
_____
_____
_____
_____
_____
_____
_____

DAILY FOCUS:

_____
_____
_____
_____
_____
_____
_____
_____
_____

NIGHTLY SUCCESS RECAP: _____
_____
_____
_____
_____
_____

NIGHTLY GRATITUDE: _____
_____
_____
_____
_____
_____

March 24

DAILY FOCUS: _____

DAILY COMMITMENT: _____
_____
_____

DAILY TOP TARGET: _____
_____
_____
_____

DAILY FOCUSED MEDITATION:

"I breathe in _____, I breathe out _____."

DAILY GOALS:	**DAILY FOCUS:**
_____	_____
_____	_____
_____	_____
_____	_____
_____	_____
_____	_____
_____	_____
_____	_____
_____	_____
_____	_____

NIGHTLY SUCCESS RECAP: _____
_____
_____
_____
_____
_____
_____

NIGHTLY GRATITUDE:_____
_____
_____
_____
_____
_____
_____

March 25

DAILY FOCUS: _____

DAILY COMMITMENT: _____
_____
_____

DAILY TOP TARGET: _____
_____
_____
_____

DAILY FOCUSED MEDITATION:

"I breathe in _____, I breathe out _____."

DAILY GOALS:

_____
_____
_____
_____
_____
_____
_____
_____
_____

DAILY FOCUS:

_____
_____
_____
_____
_____
_____
_____
_____
_____

NIGHTLY SUCCESS RECAP: _____
_____
_____
_____
_____
_____

NIGHTLY GRATITUDE:_____
_____
_____
_____
_____
_____
_____

March 26

DAILY FOCUS: _____

DAILY COMMITMENT: _____
_____
_____

DAILY TOP TARGET: _____
_____
_____
_____

DAILY FOCUSED MEDITATION:

"I breathe in _____, I breathe out _____."

DAILY GOALS:	**DAILY FOCUS:**
_____	_____
_____	_____
_____	_____
_____	_____
_____	_____
_____	_____
_____	_____
_____	_____
_____	_____
_____	_____

NIGHTLY SUCCESS RECAP: _____
_____
_____
_____
_____
_____
_____

NIGHTLY GRATITUDE: _____
_____
_____
_____
_____
_____
_____

March 27

DAILY FOCUS: _____

DAILY COMMITMENT: _____
_____
_____

DAILY TOP TARGET: _____
_____
_____
_____

DAILY FOCUSED MEDITATION:

"I breathe in _____, I breathe out _____."

DAILY GOALS:	**DAILY FOCUS:**
_____	_____
_____	_____
_____	_____
_____	_____
_____	_____
_____	_____
_____	_____
_____	_____
_____	_____

NIGHTLY SUCCESS RECAP: _____
_____
_____
_____
_____
_____
_____

NIGHTLY GRATITUDE: _____
_____
_____
_____
_____
_____
_____

DAILY FOCUS: _____

DAILY COMMITMENT: _____
_____
_____

DAILY TOP TARGET: _____
_____
_____
_____

DAILY FOCUSED MEDITATION:

"I breathe in _____, I breathe out _____."

DAILY GOALS:	**DAILY FOCUS:**
_____	_____
_____	_____
_____	_____
_____	_____
_____	_____
_____	_____
_____	_____
_____	_____
_____	_____

NIGHTLY SUCCESS RECAP: _____
_____
_____
_____
_____
_____

NIGHTLY GRATITUDE: _____
_____
_____
_____
_____
_____

March 29

DAILY FOCUS: _____

DAILY COMMITMENT: _____
_____
_____

DAILY TOP TARGET: _____
_____
_____
_____

DAILY FOCUSED MEDITATION:

"I breathe in _____, I breathe out _____."

DAILY GOALS:	**DAILY FOCUS:**
_____	_____
_____	_____
_____	_____
_____	_____
_____	_____
_____	_____
_____	_____
_____	_____
_____	_____

NIGHTLY SUCCESS RECAP: _____
_____
_____
_____
_____
_____

NIGHTLY GRATITUDE: _____
_____
_____
_____
_____
_____

March 30

DAILY FOCUS: _____

DAILY COMMITMENT: _____
_____
_____

DAILY TOP TARGET: _____
_____
_____
_____

DAILY FOCUSED MEDITATION:

"I breathe in _____, I breathe out _____."

DAILY GOALS:

_____
_____
_____
_____
_____
_____
_____
_____
_____

DAILY FOCUS:

_____
_____
_____
_____
_____
_____
_____
_____
_____

NIGHTLY SUCCESS RECAP: _____
_____
_____
_____
_____
_____
_____

NIGHTLY GRATITUDE: _____
_____
_____
_____
_____
_____
_____

March 31

DAILY FOCUS: _____

DAILY COMMITMENT: _____
_____
_____

DAILY TOP TARGET: _____
_____
_____
_____

DAILY FOCUSED MEDITATION:

"I breathe in _____, I breathe out _____."

DAILY GOALS:

_____
_____
_____
_____
_____
_____
_____
_____
_____

DAILY FOCUS:

_____
_____
_____
_____
_____
_____
_____
_____
_____

NIGHTLY SUCCESS RECAP: _____
_____
_____
_____
_____
_____

NIGHTLY GRATITUDE:_____
_____
_____
_____
_____
_____

DAILY FOCUS: _____

DAILY COMMITMENT: _____
_____
_____

DAILY TOP TARGET: _____
_____
_____
_____

DAILY FOCUSED MEDITATION:

"I breathe in _____, I breathe out _____."

DAILY GOALS:	**DAILY FOCUS:**
_____	_____
_____	_____
_____	_____
_____	_____
_____	_____
_____	_____
_____	_____
_____	_____
_____	_____
_____	_____

NIGHTLY SUCCESS RECAP: _____
_____
_____
_____
_____
_____

NIGHTLY GRATITUDE: _____
_____
_____
_____
_____
_____

April 2

DAILY FOCUS: _____

DAILY COMMITMENT: _____
_____
_____

DAILY TOP TARGET: _____
_____
_____
_____

DAILY FOCUSED MEDITATION:

"I breathe in _____, I breathe out _____."

DAILY GOALS:	**DAILY FOCUS:**
_____	_____
_____	_____
_____	_____
_____	_____
_____	_____
_____	_____
_____	_____
_____	_____
_____	_____

NIGHTLY SUCCESS RECAP: _____
_____
_____
_____
_____
_____
_____

NIGHTLY GRATITUDE: _____
_____
_____
_____
_____
_____
_____

DAILY FOCUS: _____

DAILY COMMITMENT: _____
_____
_____

DAILY TOP TARGET: _____
_____
_____
_____

DAILY FOCUSED MEDITATION:

"I breathe in _____, I breathe out _____."

DAILY GOALS:	**DAILY FOCUS:**
_____	_____
_____	_____
_____	_____
_____	_____
_____	_____
_____	_____
_____	_____
_____	_____
_____	_____
_____	_____

NIGHTLY SUCCESS RECAP: _____
_____
_____
_____
_____
_____

NIGHTLY GRATITUDE: _____
_____
_____
_____
_____
_____

April 4

DAILY FOCUS: _____

DAILY COMMITMENT: _____
_____
_____

DAILY TOP TARGET: _____
_____
_____
_____

DAILY FOCUSED MEDITATION:

"I breathe in _____, I breathe out _____."

DAILY GOALS:	DAILY FOCUS:

NIGHTLY SUCCESS RECAP: _____
_____
_____
_____
_____
_____
_____

NIGHTLY GRATITUDE:_____
_____
_____
_____
_____
_____

April 5

DAILY FOCUS: _____

DAILY COMMITMENT: _____
_____
_____

DAILY TOP TARGET: _____
_____
_____
_____

DAILY FOCUSED MEDITATION:

"I breathe in _____, I breathe out _____."

DAILY GOALS:	**DAILY FOCUS:**
_____	_____
_____	_____
_____	_____
_____	_____
_____	_____
_____	_____
_____	_____
_____	_____
_____	_____

NIGHTLY SUCCESS RECAP: _____
_____
_____
_____
_____
_____

NIGHTLY GRATITUDE: _____
_____
_____
_____
_____
_____

April 6

DAILY FOCUS: _____

DAILY COMMITMENT: _____
_____
_____

DAILY TOP TARGET: _____
_____
_____
_____

DAILY FOCUSED MEDITATION:

"I breathe in _____, I breathe out _____."

DAILY GOALS:	**DAILY FOCUS:**
_____	_____
_____	_____
_____	_____
_____	_____
_____	_____
_____	_____
_____	_____
_____	_____
_____	_____

NIGHTLY SUCCESS RECAP: _____
_____
_____
_____
_____
_____
_____

NIGHTLY GRATITUDE: _____
_____
_____
_____
_____
_____
_____

DAILY FOCUS: _____

DAILY COMMITMENT: _____
_____
_____

DAILY TOP TARGET: _____
_____
_____
_____

DAILY FOCUSED MEDITATION:

"I breathe in _____, I breathe out _____."

DAILY GOALS:	**DAILY FOCUS:**
_____	_____
_____	_____
_____	_____
_____	_____
_____	_____
_____	_____
_____	_____
_____	_____
_____	_____

NIGHTLY SUCCESS RECAP: _____
_____
_____
_____
_____
_____

NIGHTLY GRATITUDE: _____
_____
_____
_____
_____
_____

April 8

DAILY FOCUS: _____

DAILY COMMITMENT: _____
_____
_____

DAILY TOP TARGET: _____
_____
_____
_____

DAILY FOCUSED MEDITATION:

"I breathe in _____, I breathe out _____."

DAILY GOALS:	DAILY FOCUS:
_____	_____
_____	_____
_____	_____
_____	_____
_____	_____
_____	_____
_____	_____
_____	_____
_____	_____

NIGHTLY SUCCESS RECAP: _____
_____
_____
_____
_____
_____
_____

NIGHTLY GRATITUDE:_____
_____
_____
_____
_____
_____
_____

DAILY FOCUS: _____

DAILY COMMITMENT: _____
_____
_____

DAILY TOP TARGET: _____
_____
_____
_____

DAILY FOCUSED MEDITATION:

"I breathe in _____, I breathe out _____."

DAILY GOALS: **DAILY FOCUS:**

_____   _____
_____   _____
_____   _____
_____   _____
_____   _____
_____   _____
_____   _____
_____   _____
_____   _____

NIGHTLY SUCCESS RECAP: _____
_____
_____
_____
_____
_____
_____

NIGHTLY GRATITUDE: _____
_____
_____
_____
_____
_____
_____

April 10

DAILY FOCUS: _____

DAILY COMMITMENT: _____
_____
_____

DAILY TOP TARGET: _____
_____
_____
_____

DAILY FOCUSED MEDITATION:

"I breathe in _____, I breathe out _____."

DAILY GOALS:	**DAILY FOCUS:**
_____	_____
_____	_____
_____	_____
_____	_____
_____	_____
_____	_____
_____	_____
_____	_____
_____	_____

NIGHTLY SUCCESS RECAP: _____
_____
_____
_____
_____
_____
_____

NIGHTLY GRATITUDE: _____
_____
_____
_____
_____
_____
_____

DAILY FOCUS: _____

DAILY COMMITMENT: _____
_____
_____

DAILY TOP TARGET: _____
_____
_____
_____

DAILY FOCUSED MEDITATION:

"I breathe in _____, I breathe out _____."

DAILY GOALS:	**DAILY FOCUS:**
_____	_____
_____	_____
_____	_____
_____	_____
_____	_____
_____	_____
_____	_____
_____	_____
_____	_____

NIGHTLY SUCCESS RECAP: _____
_____
_____
_____
_____
_____
_____

NIGHTLY GRATITUDE: _____
_____
_____
_____
_____
_____
_____

April 12

DAILY FOCUS: _____

DAILY COMMITMENT: _____
_____
_____

DAILY TOP TARGET: _____
_____
_____
_____

DAILY FOCUSED MEDITATION:

"I breathe in _____, I breathe out _____."

DAILY GOALS:	**DAILY FOCUS:**
_____	_____
_____	_____
_____	_____
_____	_____
_____	_____
_____	_____
_____	_____
_____	_____

NIGHTLY SUCCESS RECAP: _____
_____
_____
_____
_____
_____

NIGHTLY GRATITUDE: _____
_____
_____
_____
_____
_____

DAILY FOCUS: _____

DAILY COMMITMENT: _____
_____
_____

DAILY TOP TARGET: _____
_____
_____
_____

DAILY FOCUSED MEDITATION:

"I breathe in _____, I breathe out _____."

DAILY GOALS: **DAILY FOCUS:**

_____   _____
_____   _____
_____   _____
_____   _____
_____   _____
_____   _____
_____   _____
_____   _____
_____   _____

NIGHTLY SUCCESS RECAP: _____
_____
_____
_____
_____
_____

NIGHTLY GRATITUDE: _____
_____
_____
_____
_____
_____

April 14

DAILY FOCUS: _____

DAILY COMMITMENT: _____
_____
_____

DAILY TOP TARGET: _____
_____
_____
_____

DAILY FOCUSED MEDITATION:

"I breathe in _____, I breathe out _____."

DAILY GOALS:	**DAILY FOCUS:**
_____	_____
_____	_____
_____	_____
_____	_____
_____	_____
_____	_____
_____	_____
_____	_____
_____	_____

NIGHTLY SUCCESS RECAP: _____
_____
_____
_____
_____
_____

NIGHTLY GRATITUDE:_____
_____
_____
_____
_____
_____
_____

April 15

DAILY FOCUS: _____

DAILY COMMITMENT: _____
_____
_____

DAILY TOP TARGET: _____
_____
_____
_____

DAILY FOCUSED MEDITATION:

"I breathe in _____, I breathe out _____."

DAILY GOALS:	**DAILY FOCUS:**

NIGHTLY SUCCESS RECAP: _____
_____
_____
_____
_____
_____
_____

NIGHTLY GRATITUDE:_____
_____
_____
_____
_____
_____
_____

April 16

DAILY FOCUS: _____

DAILY COMMITMENT: _____
_____
_____

DAILY TOP TARGET: _____
_____
_____
_____

DAILY FOCUSED MEDITATION:

"I breathe in _____, I breathe out _____."

DAILY GOALS: DAILY FOCUS:

_____   _____
_____   _____
_____   _____
_____   _____
_____   _____
_____   _____
_____   _____
_____   _____

NIGHTLY SUCCESS RECAP: _____
_____
_____
_____
_____
_____

NIGHTLY GRATITUDE:_____
_____
_____
_____
_____
_____
_____

DAILY FOCUS: _____

DAILY COMMITMENT: _____
_____
_____

DAILY TOP TARGET: _____
_____
_____
_____

DAILY FOCUSED MEDITATION:

"I breathe in _____, I breathe out _____."

DAILY GOALS:

_____
_____
_____
_____
_____
_____
_____
_____

DAILY FOCUS:

_____
_____
_____
_____
_____
_____
_____
_____

NIGHTLY SUCCESS RECAP: _____
_____
_____
_____
_____
_____
_____

NIGHTLY GRATITUDE: _____
_____
_____
_____
_____
_____
_____

April 18

DAILY FOCUS: _____

DAILY COMMITMENT: _____
_____
_____

DAILY TOP TARGET: _____
_____
_____
_____

DAILY FOCUSED MEDITATION:

"I breathe in _____, I breathe out _____."

DAILY GOALS:	DAILY FOCUS:
_____	_____
_____	_____
_____	_____
_____	_____
_____	_____
_____	_____
_____	_____
_____	_____

NIGHTLY SUCCESS RECAP: _____
_____
_____
_____
_____
_____
_____

NIGHTLY GRATITUDE:_____
_____
_____
_____
_____
_____
_____
_____

DAILY FOCUS: _____

DAILY COMMITMENT: _____
_____
_____

DAILY TOP TARGET: _____
_____
_____
_____

DAILY FOCUSED MEDITATION:

"I breathe in _____, I breathe out _____."

DAILY GOALS:	**DAILY FOCUS:**
_____	_____
_____	_____
_____	_____
_____	_____
_____	_____
_____	_____
_____	_____
_____	_____
_____	_____
_____	_____

NIGHTLY SUCCESS RECAP: _____
_____
_____
_____
_____
_____

NIGHTLY GRATITUDE: _____
_____
_____
_____
_____
_____

April 20

DAILY FOCUS: _____

DAILY COMMITMENT: _____
_____
_____

DAILY TOP TARGET: _____
_____
_____
_____

DAILY FOCUSED MEDITATION:

"I breathe in _____, I breathe out _____."

DAILY GOALS:	**DAILY FOCUS:**
_____	_____
_____	_____
_____	_____
_____	_____
_____	_____
_____	_____
_____	_____
_____	_____
_____	_____

NIGHTLY SUCCESS RECAP: _____
_____
_____
_____
_____
_____

NIGHTLY GRATITUDE: _____
_____
_____
_____
_____
_____
_____

DAILY FOCUS: _____

DAILY COMMITMENT: _____
_____
_____

DAILY TOP TARGET: _____
_____
_____
_____

DAILY FOCUSED MEDITATION:

"I breathe in _____, I breathe out _____."

DAILY GOALS: **DAILY FOCUS:**

_____   _____
_____   _____
_____   _____
_____   _____
_____   _____
_____   _____
_____   _____
_____   _____
_____   _____

NIGHTLY SUCCESS RECAP: _____
_____
_____
_____
_____
_____
_____

NIGHTLY GRATITUDE: _____
_____
_____
_____
_____
_____
_____

April 22

DAILY FOCUS: _____

DAILY COMMITMENT: _____
_____
_____

DAILY TOP TARGET: _____
_____
_____
_____

DAILY FOCUSED MEDITATION:

"I breathe in _____, I breathe out _____."

DAILY GOALS:	DAILY FOCUS:

NIGHTLY SUCCESS RECAP: _____
_____
_____
_____
_____
_____

NIGHTLY GRATITUDE: _____
_____
_____
_____
_____
_____

April 23

DAILY FOCUS: _____

DAILY COMMITMENT: _____
_____
_____

DAILY TOP TARGET: _____
_____
_____
_____

DAILY FOCUSED MEDITATION:

"I breathe in _____, I breathe out _____."

DAILY GOALS: **DAILY FOCUS:**

_____   _____
_____   _____
_____   _____
_____   _____
_____   _____
_____   _____
_____   _____
_____   _____
_____   _____

NIGHTLY SUCCESS RECAP: _____
_____
_____
_____
_____
_____

NIGHTLY GRATITUDE: _____
_____
_____
_____
_____
_____
_____

April 24

DAILY FOCUS: _____

DAILY COMMITMENT: _____
_____
_____

DAILY TOP TARGET: _____
_____
_____
_____

DAILY FOCUSED MEDITATION:

"I breathe in _____, I breathe out _____."

<table>
<tr><td align="center">DAILY GOALS:</td><td align="center">DAILY FOCUS:</td></tr>
</table>

DAILY GOALS:

_____
_____
_____
_____
_____
_____
_____
_____

DAILY FOCUS:

_____
_____
_____
_____
_____
_____
_____
_____

NIGHTLY SUCCESS RECAP: _____
_____
_____
_____
_____
_____
_____

NIGHTLY GRATITUDE:_____
_____
_____
_____
_____
_____
_____

DAILY FOCUS: _____

DAILY COMMITMENT: _____
_____
_____

DAILY TOP TARGET: _____
_____
_____
_____

DAILY FOCUSED MEDITATION:

"I breathe in _____, I breathe out _____."

DAILY GOALS: **DAILY FOCUS:**

_____   _____
_____   _____
_____   _____
_____   _____
_____   _____
_____   _____
_____   _____
_____   _____
_____   _____

NIGHTLY SUCCESS RECAP: _____
_____
_____
_____
_____
_____

NIGHTLY GRATITUDE: _____
_____
_____
_____
_____
_____

April 26

DAILY FOCUS: _____

DAILY COMMITMENT: _____
_____
_____

DAILY TOP TARGET: _____
_____
_____
_____

DAILY FOCUSED MEDITATION:

"I breathe in _____, I breathe out _____."

DAILY GOALS: **DAILY FOCUS:**

_____ _____
_____ _____
_____ _____
_____ _____
_____ _____
_____ _____
_____ _____
_____ _____

NIGHTLY SUCCESS RECAP: _____
_____
_____
_____
_____
_____
_____

NIGHTLY GRATITUDE: _____
_____
_____
_____
_____
_____
_____

DAILY FOCUS: _____

DAILY COMMITMENT: _____
_____
_____

DAILY TOP TARGET: _____
_____
_____
_____

DAILY FOCUSED MEDITATION:

"I breathe in _____, I breathe out _____."

DAILY GOALS: **DAILY FOCUS:**

_____   _____
_____   _____
_____   _____
_____   _____
_____   _____
_____   _____
_____   _____
_____   _____
_____   _____

NIGHTLY SUCCESS RECAP: _____
_____
_____
_____
_____
_____

NIGHTLY GRATITUDE: _____
_____
_____
_____
_____
_____

April 28

DAILY FOCUS: _____

DAILY COMMITMENT: _____
_____
_____

DAILY TOP TARGET: _____
_____
_____
_____

DAILY FOCUSED MEDITATION:

"I breathe in _____, I breathe out _____."

DAILY GOALS: DAILY FOCUS:

_____   _____
_____   _____
_____   _____
_____   _____
_____   _____
_____   _____
_____   _____
_____   _____
_____   _____

NIGHTLY SUCCESS RECAP: _____
_____
_____
_____
_____
_____
_____

NIGHTLY GRATITUDE:_____
_____
_____
_____
_____
_____
_____
_____

DAILY FOCUS: _____

DAILY COMMITMENT: _____
_____
_____

DAILY TOP TARGET: _____
_____
_____
_____

DAILY FOCUSED MEDITATION:

"I breathe in _____, I breathe out _____."

DAILY GOALS:	**DAILY FOCUS:**
_____	_____
_____	_____
_____	_____
_____	_____
_____	_____
_____	_____
_____	_____
_____	_____
_____	_____

NIGHTLY SUCCESS RECAP: _____
_____
_____
_____
_____
_____
_____

NIGHTLY GRATITUDE: _____
_____
_____
_____
_____
_____

April 30

DAILY FOCUS: _____

DAILY COMMITMENT: _____
_____
_____

DAILY TOP TARGET: _____
_____
_____
_____

DAILY FOCUSED MEDITATION:

"I breathe in _____, I breathe out _____."

DAILY GOALS: DAILY FOCUS:

_____   _____
_____   _____
_____   _____
_____   _____
_____   _____
_____   _____
_____   _____
_____   _____
_____   _____
_____   _____

NIGHTLY SUCCESS RECAP: _____
_____
_____
_____
_____
_____
_____

NIGHTLY GRATITUDE: _____
_____
_____
_____
_____
_____
_____

May 1

DAILY FOCUS: _____

DAILY COMMITMENT: _____
_____
_____

DAILY TOP TARGET: _____
_____
_____
_____

DAILY FOCUSED MEDITATION:

"I breathe in _____, I breathe out _____."

DAILY GOALS:	**DAILY FOCUS:**
_____	_____
_____	_____
_____	_____
_____	_____
_____	_____
_____	_____
_____	_____
_____	_____
_____	_____

NIGHTLY SUCCESS RECAP: _____
_____
_____
_____
_____
_____

NIGHTLY GRATITUDE: _____
_____
_____
_____
_____
_____
_____

May 2

DAILY FOCUS: _____

DAILY COMMITMENT: _____
_____
_____

DAILY TOP TARGET: _____
_____
_____
_____

DAILY FOCUSED MEDITATION:

"I breathe in _____, I breathe out _____."

<table>
<tr><td align="center">DAILY GOALS:</td><td align="center">DAILY FOCUS:</td></tr>
</table>

DAILY GOALS:	DAILY FOCUS:
_____	_____
_____	_____
_____	_____
_____	_____
_____	_____
_____	_____
_____	_____
_____	_____
_____	_____
_____	_____

NIGHTLY SUCCESS RECAP: _____
_____
_____
_____
_____
_____

NIGHTLY GRATITUDE: _____
_____
_____
_____
_____
_____

DAILY FOCUS: _____

DAILY COMMITMENT: _____
_____
_____

DAILY TOP TARGET: _____
_____
_____
_____

DAILY FOCUSED MEDITATION:

"I breathe in _____, I breathe out _____."

DAILY GOALS:	**DAILY FOCUS:**
_____	_____
_____	_____
_____	_____
_____	_____
_____	_____
_____	_____
_____	_____
_____	_____
_____	_____
_____	_____

NIGHTLY SUCCESS RECAP: _____
_____
_____
_____
_____
_____

NIGHTLY GRATITUDE: _____
_____
_____
_____
_____
_____

May 4

DAILY FOCUS: _____

DAILY COMMITMENT: _____
_____
_____

DAILY TOP TARGET: _____
_____
_____
_____

DAILY FOCUSED MEDITATION:

"I breathe in _____, I breathe out _____."

DAILY GOALS: **DAILY FOCUS:**

_____   _____
_____   _____
_____   _____
_____   _____
_____   _____
_____   _____
_____   _____
_____   _____

NIGHTLY SUCCESS RECAP: _____
_____
_____
_____
_____
_____

NIGHTLY GRATITUDE: _____
_____
_____
_____
_____
_____
_____

DAILY FOCUS: _____

DAILY COMMITMENT: _____
_____
_____

DAILY TOP TARGET: _____
_____
_____
_____

DAILY FOCUSED MEDITATION:

"I breathe in _____, I breathe out _____."

DAILY GOALS:

_____
_____
_____
_____
_____
_____
_____
_____
_____

DAILY FOCUS:

_____
_____
_____
_____
_____
_____
_____
_____
_____

NIGHTLY SUCCESS RECAP: _____
_____
_____
_____
_____
_____
_____

NIGHTLY GRATITUDE: _____
_____
_____
_____
_____
_____
_____

May 6

DAILY FOCUS: _____

DAILY COMMITMENT: _____
_____
_____

DAILY TOP TARGET: _____
_____
_____
_____

DAILY FOCUSED MEDITATION:

"I breathe in _____, I breathe out _____."

DAILY GOALS: DAILY FOCUS:

_____   _____
_____   _____
_____   _____
_____   _____
_____   _____
_____   _____
_____   _____
_____   _____
_____   _____

NIGHTLY SUCCESS RECAP: _____
_____
_____
_____
_____
_____
_____

NIGHTLY GRATITUDE: _____
_____
_____
_____
_____
_____
_____

DAILY FOCUS: _____

DAILY COMMITMENT: _____
_____
_____

DAILY TOP TARGET: _____
_____
_____
_____

DAILY FOCUSED MEDITATION:

"I breathe in _____, I breathe out _____."

DAILY GOALS: **DAILY FOCUS:**

_____   _____
_____   _____
_____   _____
_____   _____
_____   _____
_____   _____
_____   _____
_____   _____
_____   _____

NIGHTLY SUCCESS RECAP: _____
_____
_____
_____
_____
_____

NIGHTLY GRATITUDE: _____
_____
_____
_____
_____
_____

May 8

DAILY FOCUS: _____

DAILY COMMITMENT: _____
_____
_____

DAILY TOP TARGET: _____
_____
_____
_____

DAILY FOCUSED MEDITATION:

"I breathe in _____, I breathe out _____."

<table>
<tr><td align="center">DAILY GOALS:</td><td align="center">DAILY FOCUS:</td></tr>
</table>

DAILY GOALS:	DAILY FOCUS:
_____	_____
_____	_____
_____	_____
_____	_____
_____	_____
_____	_____
_____	_____
_____	_____
_____	_____

NIGHTLY SUCCESS RECAP: _____
_____
_____
_____
_____
_____

NIGHTLY GRATITUDE: _____
_____
_____
_____
_____
_____
_____

DAILY FOCUS: _____

DAILY COMMITMENT: _____
_____
_____

DAILY TOP TARGET: _____
_____
_____
_____

DAILY FOCUSED MEDITATION:

"I breathe in _____, I breathe out _____."

DAILY GOALS:	**DAILY FOCUS:**
_____	_____
_____	_____
_____	_____
_____	_____
_____	_____
_____	_____
_____	_____
_____	_____
_____	_____
_____	_____

NIGHTLY SUCCESS RECAP: _____
_____
_____
_____
_____
_____
_____

NIGHTLY GRATITUDE: _____
_____
_____
_____
_____
_____
_____

May 10

DAILY FOCUS: _____

DAILY COMMITMENT: _____
_____
_____

DAILY TOP TARGET: _____
_____
_____
_____

DAILY FOCUSED MEDITATION:

"I breathe in _____, I breathe out _____."

<table>
<tr><td align="center">DAILY GOALS:</td><td align="center">DAILY FOCUS:</td></tr>
</table>

DAILY GOALS:	DAILY FOCUS:
_____	_____
_____	_____
_____	_____
_____	_____
_____	_____
_____	_____
_____	_____
_____	_____
_____	_____

NIGHTLY SUCCESS RECAP: _____
_____
_____
_____
_____
_____
_____

NIGHTLY GRATITUDE:_____
_____
_____
_____
_____
_____
_____

DAILY FOCUS: _____

DAILY COMMITMENT: _____
_____
_____

DAILY TOP TARGET: _____
_____
_____
_____

DAILY FOCUSED MEDITATION:

"I breathe in _____, I breathe out _____."

DAILY GOALS:

_____
_____
_____
_____
_____
_____
_____
_____
_____

DAILY FOCUS:

_____
_____
_____
_____
_____
_____
_____
_____
_____

NIGHTLY SUCCESS RECAP: _____
_____
_____
_____
_____
_____
_____

NIGHTLY GRATITUDE: _____
_____
_____
_____
_____
_____
_____

May 12

DAILY FOCUS: _____

DAILY COMMITMENT: _____
_____
_____

DAILY TOP TARGET: _____
_____
_____
_____

DAILY FOCUSED MEDITATION:

"I breathe in _____, I breathe out _____."

DAILY GOALS:	**DAILY FOCUS:**
_____	_____
_____	_____
_____	_____
_____	_____
_____	_____
_____	_____
_____	_____
_____	_____
_____	_____

NIGHTLY SUCCESS RECAP: _____
_____
_____
_____
_____
_____
_____

NIGHTLY GRATITUDE: _____
_____
_____
_____
_____
_____
_____
_____

DAILY FOCUS: _____

DAILY COMMITMENT: _____
_____
_____

DAILY TOP TARGET: _____
_____
_____
_____

DAILY FOCUSED MEDITATION:

"I breathe in _____, I breathe out _____."

DAILY GOALS:	**DAILY FOCUS:**
_____	_____
_____	_____
_____	_____
_____	_____
_____	_____
_____	_____
_____	_____
_____	_____
_____	_____

NIGHTLY SUCCESS RECAP: _____
_____
_____
_____
_____
_____

NIGHTLY GRATITUDE: _____
_____
_____
_____
_____
_____

May 14

DAILY FOCUS: _____

DAILY COMMITMENT: _____
_____
_____

DAILY TOP TARGET: _____
_____
_____
_____

DAILY FOCUSED MEDITATION:

"I breathe in _____, I breathe out _____."

DAILY GOALS:	DAILY FOCUS:
_____	_____
_____	_____
_____	_____
_____	_____
_____	_____
_____	_____
_____	_____
_____	_____

NIGHTLY SUCCESS RECAP: _____
_____
_____
_____
_____
_____

NIGHTLY GRATITUDE: _____
_____
_____
_____
_____
_____
_____

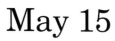

DAILY FOCUS: _____

DAILY COMMITMENT: _____
_____
_____

DAILY TOP TARGET: _____
_____
_____
_____

DAILY FOCUSED MEDITATION:

"I breathe in _____, I breathe out _____."

DAILY GOALS: **DAILY FOCUS:**

_____   _____
_____   _____
_____   _____
_____   _____
_____   _____
_____   _____
_____   _____
_____   _____
_____   _____
_____   _____

NIGHTLY SUCCESS RECAP: _____
_____
_____
_____
_____
_____

NIGHTLY GRATITUDE: _____
_____
_____
_____
_____
_____
_____

May 16

DAILY FOCUS: _____

DAILY COMMITMENT: _____
_____
_____

DAILY TOP TARGET: _____
_____
_____
_____

DAILY FOCUSED MEDITATION:

"I breathe in _____, I breathe out _____."

DAILY GOALS:	**DAILY FOCUS:**
_____	_____
_____	_____
_____	_____
_____	_____
_____	_____
_____	_____
_____	_____
_____	_____
_____	_____

NIGHTLY SUCCESS RECAP: _____
_____
_____
_____
_____
_____

NIGHTLY GRATITUDE: _____
_____
_____
_____
_____
_____

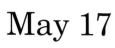
May 17

DAILY FOCUS: _____

DAILY COMMITMENT: _____
_____
_____

DAILY TOP TARGET: _____
_____
_____
_____

DAILY FOCUSED MEDITATION:

"I breathe in _____, I breathe out _____."

DAILY GOALS:	**DAILY FOCUS:**
_____	_____
_____	_____
_____	_____
_____	_____
_____	_____
_____	_____
_____	_____
_____	_____
_____	_____

NIGHTLY SUCCESS RECAP: _____
_____
_____
_____
_____
_____

NIGHTLY GRATITUDE:_____
_____
_____
_____
_____
_____
_____

May 18

DAILY FOCUS: _____

DAILY COMMITMENT: _____
_____
_____

DAILY TOP TARGET: _____
_____
_____
_____

DAILY FOCUSED MEDITATION:

"I breathe in _____, I breathe out _____."

DAILY GOALS:	**DAILY FOCUS:**
_____	_____
_____	_____
_____	_____
_____	_____
_____	_____
_____	_____
_____	_____
_____	_____
_____	_____

NIGHTLY SUCCESS RECAP: _____
_____
_____
_____
_____
_____
_____

NIGHTLY GRATITUDE: _____
_____
_____
_____
_____
_____
_____

DAILY FOCUS: _____

DAILY COMMITMENT: _____
_____
_____

DAILY TOP TARGET: _____
_____
_____
_____

DAILY FOCUSED MEDITATION:

"I breathe in _____, I breathe out _____."

DAILY GOALS: **DAILY FOCUS:**

_____   _____
_____   _____
_____   _____
_____   _____
_____   _____
_____   _____
_____   _____
_____   _____
_____   _____
_____   _____

NIGHTLY SUCCESS RECAP: _____
_____
_____
_____
_____
_____
_____

NIGHTLY GRATITUDE: _____
_____
_____
_____
_____
_____
_____

May 20

DAILY FOCUS: _____

DAILY COMMITMENT: _____
_____
_____

DAILY TOP TARGET: _____
_____
_____
_____

DAILY FOCUSED MEDITATION:

"I breathe in _____, I breathe out _____."

DAILY GOALS:	**DAILY FOCUS:**
_____	_____
_____	_____
_____	_____
_____	_____
_____	_____
_____	_____
_____	_____
_____	_____
_____	_____

NIGHTLY SUCCESS RECAP: _____
_____
_____
_____
_____
_____

NIGHTLY GRATITUDE:_____
_____
_____
_____
_____
_____

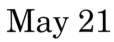
May 21

DAILY FOCUS: _____

DAILY COMMITMENT: _____
_____
_____

DAILY TOP TARGET: _____
_____
_____
_____

DAILY FOCUSED MEDITATION:

"I breathe in _____, I breathe out _____."

DAILY GOALS: **DAILY FOCUS:**

_____   _____
_____   _____
_____   _____
_____   _____
_____   _____
_____   _____
_____   _____
_____   _____
_____   _____

NIGHTLY SUCCESS RECAP: _____
_____
_____
_____
_____
_____

NIGHTLY GRATITUDE: _____
_____
_____
_____
_____
_____
_____

May 22

DAILY FOCUS: _____

DAILY COMMITMENT: _____
_____
_____

DAILY TOP TARGET: _____
_____
_____
_____

DAILY FOCUSED MEDITATION:

"I breathe in _____, I breathe out _____."

       DAILY GOALS: DAILY FOCUS:

_____	_____
_____	_____
_____	_____
_____	_____
_____	_____
_____	_____
_____	_____
_____	_____
_____	_____

NIGHTLY SUCCESS RECAP: _____
_____
_____
_____
_____
_____

NIGHTLY GRATITUDE:_____
_____
_____
_____
_____
_____
_____

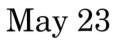

DAILY FOCUS: _____

DAILY COMMITMENT: _____
_____
_____

DAILY TOP TARGET: _____
_____
_____
_____

DAILY FOCUSED MEDITATION:

"I breathe in _____, I breathe out _____."

DAILY GOALS:	**DAILY FOCUS:**
_____	_____
_____	_____
_____	_____
_____	_____
_____	_____
_____	_____
_____	_____
_____	_____
_____	_____

NIGHTLY SUCCESS RECAP: _____
_____
_____
_____
_____
_____
_____

NIGHTLY GRATITUDE: _____
_____
_____
_____
_____
_____
_____

May 24

DAILY FOCUS: _____

DAILY COMMITMENT: _____
_____
_____

DAILY TOP TARGET: _____
_____
_____
_____

DAILY FOCUSED MEDITATION:

"I breathe in _____, I breathe out _____."

DAILY GOALS: DAILY FOCUS:

_____   _____
_____   _____
_____   _____
_____   _____
_____   _____
_____   _____
_____   _____
_____   _____
_____   _____

NIGHTLY SUCCESS RECAP: _____
_____
_____
_____
_____
_____

NIGHTLY GRATITUDE: _____
_____
_____
_____
_____
_____

DAILY FOCUS: _____

DAILY COMMITMENT: _____
_____
_____

DAILY TOP TARGET: _____
_____
_____
_____

DAILY FOCUSED MEDITATION:

"I breathe in _____, I breathe out _____."

DAILY GOALS: **DAILY FOCUS:**

_____   _____
_____   _____
_____   _____
_____   _____
_____   _____
_____   _____
_____   _____
_____   _____
_____   _____

NIGHTLY SUCCESS RECAP: _____
_____
_____
_____
_____
_____
_____

NIGHTLY GRATITUDE:_____
_____
_____
_____
_____
_____
_____

May 26

DAILY FOCUS: _____

DAILY COMMITMENT: _____
_____
_____

DAILY TOP TARGET: _____
_____
_____
_____

DAILY FOCUSED MEDITATION:

"I breathe in _____, I breathe out _____."

DAILY GOALS:

_____
_____
_____
_____
_____
_____
_____
_____
_____
_____

DAILY FOCUS:

_____
_____
_____
_____
_____
_____
_____
_____
_____
_____

NIGHTLY SUCCESS RECAP: _____
_____
_____
_____
_____
_____
_____

NIGHTLY GRATITUDE: _____
_____
_____
_____
_____
_____
_____

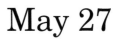

DAILY FOCUS: _____

DAILY COMMITMENT: _____
_____
_____

DAILY TOP TARGET: _____
_____
_____
_____

DAILY FOCUSED MEDITATION:

"I breathe in _____, I breathe out _____."

DAILY GOALS: **DAILY FOCUS:**

_____   _____
_____   _____
_____   _____
_____   _____
_____   _____
_____   _____
_____   _____
_____   _____
_____   _____
_____   _____

NIGHTLY SUCCESS RECAP: _____
_____
_____
_____
_____
_____

NIGHTLY GRATITUDE: _____
_____
_____
_____
_____
_____

May 28

DAILY FOCUS: _____

DAILY COMMITMENT: _____
_____
_____

DAILY TOP TARGET: _____
_____
_____
_____

DAILY FOCUSED MEDITATION:

"I breathe in _____, I breathe out _____."

DAILY GOALS:	**DAILY FOCUS:**
_____	_____
_____	_____
_____	_____
_____	_____
_____	_____
_____	_____
_____	_____
_____	_____
_____	_____

NIGHTLY SUCCESS RECAP: _____
_____
_____
_____
_____
_____
_____

NIGHTLY GRATITUDE: _____
_____
_____
_____
_____
_____
_____

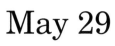

May 29

DAILY FOCUS: _____

DAILY COMMITMENT: _____
_____
_____

DAILY TOP TARGET: _____
_____
_____
_____

DAILY FOCUSED MEDITATION:

"I breathe in _____, I breathe out _____."

DAILY GOALS:	**DAILY FOCUS:**
_____	_____
_____	_____
_____	_____
_____	_____
_____	_____
_____	_____
_____	_____
_____	_____
_____	_____

NIGHTLY SUCCESS RECAP: _____
_____
_____
_____
_____
_____
_____

NIGHTLY GRATITUDE: _____
_____
_____
_____
_____
_____
_____

May 30

DAILY FOCUS: _____

DAILY COMMITMENT: _____
_____
_____

DAILY TOP TARGET: _____
_____
_____
_____

DAILY FOCUSED MEDITATION:

"I breathe in _____, I breathe out _____."

DAILY GOALS:	DAILY FOCUS:
_____	_____
_____	_____
_____	_____
_____	_____
_____	_____
_____	_____
_____	_____
_____	_____
_____	_____
_____	_____

NIGHTLY SUCCESS RECAP: _____
_____
_____
_____
_____
_____
_____

NIGHTLY GRATITUDE: _____
_____
_____
_____
_____
_____

DAILY FOCUS: _____

DAILY COMMITMENT: _____
_____
_____

DAILY TOP TARGET: _____
_____
_____
_____

DAILY FOCUSED MEDITATION:

"I breathe in _____, I breathe out _____."

DAILY GOALS:	**DAILY FOCUS:**
_____	_____
_____	_____
_____	_____
_____	_____
_____	_____
_____	_____
_____	_____
_____	_____
_____	_____

NIGHTLY SUCCESS RECAP: _____
_____
_____
_____
_____

NIGHTLY GRATITUDE: _____
_____
_____
_____
_____
_____

June 1

DAILY FOCUS: _____

DAILY COMMITMENT: _____
_____
_____

DAILY TOP TARGET: _____
_____
_____
_____

DAILY FOCUSED MEDITATION:

"I breathe in _____, I breathe out _____."

DAILY GOALS: DAILY FOCUS:

_____   _____
_____   _____
_____   _____
_____   _____
_____   _____
_____   _____
_____   _____
_____   _____

NIGHTLY SUCCESS RECAP: _____
_____
_____
_____
_____
_____
_____

NIGHTLY GRATITUDE: _____
_____
_____
_____
_____
_____
_____

DAILY FOCUS: _____

DAILY COMMITMENT: _____
_____
_____

DAILY TOP TARGET: _____
_____
_____
_____

DAILY FOCUSED MEDITATION:

"I breathe in _____, I breathe out _____."

DAILY GOALS:

_____
_____
_____
_____
_____
_____
_____
_____
_____
_____

DAILY FOCUS:

_____
_____
_____
_____
_____
_____
_____
_____
_____
_____

NIGHTLY SUCCESS RECAP: _____
_____
_____
_____
_____
_____
_____

NIGHTLY GRATITUDE: _____
_____
_____
_____
_____
_____
_____

June 3

DAILY FOCUS: _____

DAILY COMMITMENT: _____
_____
_____

DAILY TOP TARGET: _____
_____
_____
_____

DAILY FOCUSED MEDITATION:

"I breathe in _____, I breathe out _____."

DAILY GOALS: | DAILY FOCUS:

_____   _____
_____   _____
_____   _____
_____   _____
_____   _____
_____   _____
_____   _____
_____   _____
_____   _____

NIGHTLY SUCCESS RECAP: _____
_____
_____
_____
_____
_____
_____

NIGHTLY GRATITUDE: _____
_____
_____
_____
_____
_____
_____

DAILY FOCUS: _____

DAILY COMMITMENT: _____
_____
_____

DAILY TOP TARGET: _____
_____
_____
_____

DAILY FOCUSED MEDITATION:

"I breathe in _____, I breathe out _____."

DAILY GOALS:	DAILY FOCUS:
_____	_____
_____	_____
_____	_____
_____	_____
_____	_____
_____	_____
_____	_____
_____	_____
_____	_____

NIGHTLY SUCCESS RECAP: _____
_____
_____
_____
_____
_____

NIGHTLY GRATITUDE: _____
_____
_____
_____
_____
_____

June 5

DAILY FOCUS: _____

DAILY COMMITMENT: _____
_____
_____

DAILY TOP TARGET: _____
_____
_____
_____

DAILY FOCUSED MEDITATION:

"I breathe in _____, I breathe out _____."

DAILY GOALS: DAILY FOCUS:

_____   _____
_____   _____
_____   _____
_____   _____
_____   _____
_____   _____
_____   _____
_____   _____
_____   _____
_____   _____

NIGHTLY SUCCESS RECAP: _____
_____
_____
_____
_____
_____
_____

NIGHTLY GRATITUDE:_____
_____
_____
_____
_____
_____
_____

DAILY FOCUS: _____

DAILY COMMITMENT: _____
_____
_____

DAILY TOP TARGET: _____
_____
_____
_____

DAILY FOCUSED MEDITATION:

"I breathe in _____, I breathe out _____."

DAILY GOALS:	DAILY FOCUS:
_____	_____
_____	_____
_____	_____
_____	_____
_____	_____
_____	_____
_____	_____
_____	_____
_____	_____

NIGHTLY SUCCESS RECAP: _____
_____
_____
_____
_____
_____
_____

NIGHTLY GRATITUDE: _____
_____
_____
_____
_____
_____
_____

June 7

DAILY FOCUS: _____

DAILY COMMITMENT: _____
_____
_____

DAILY TOP TARGET: _____
_____
_____
_____

DAILY FOCUSED MEDITATION:

"I breathe in _____, I breathe out _____."

DAILY GOALS:

_____
_____
_____
_____
_____
_____
_____
_____
_____

DAILY FOCUS:

_____
_____
_____
_____
_____
_____
_____
_____
_____

NIGHTLY SUCCESS RECAP: _____
_____
_____
_____
_____
_____
_____

NIGHTLY GRATITUDE:_____
_____
_____
_____
_____
_____
_____

DAILY FOCUS: _____

DAILY COMMITMENT: _____
_____
_____

DAILY TOP TARGET: _____
_____
_____
_____

DAILY FOCUSED MEDITATION:

"I breathe in _____, I breathe out _____."

DAILY GOALS:	**DAILY FOCUS:**
_____	_____
_____	_____
_____	_____
_____	_____
_____	_____
_____	_____
_____	_____
_____	_____
_____	_____

NIGHTLY SUCCESS RECAP: _____
_____
_____
_____
_____
_____

NIGHTLY GRATITUDE: _____
_____
_____
_____
_____
_____
_____

June 9

DAILY FOCUS: _____

DAILY COMMITMENT: _____
_____
_____

DAILY TOP TARGET: _____
_____
_____
_____

DAILY FOCUSED MEDITATION:

"I breathe in _____, I breathe out _____."

DAILY GOALS:

_____
_____
_____
_____
_____
_____
_____
_____
_____

DAILY FOCUS:

_____
_____
_____
_____
_____
_____
_____
_____
_____

NIGHTLY SUCCESS RECAP: _____
_____
_____
_____
_____
_____
_____

NIGHTLY GRATITUDE: _____
_____
_____
_____
_____
_____
_____

DAILY FOCUS: _____

DAILY COMMITMENT: _____
_____
_____

DAILY TOP TARGET: _____
_____
_____
_____

DAILY FOCUSED MEDITATION:

"I breathe in _____, I breathe out _____."

DAILY GOALS: **DAILY FOCUS:**

_____   _____
_____   _____
_____   _____
_____   _____
_____   _____
_____   _____
_____   _____
_____   _____
_____   _____

NIGHTLY SUCCESS RECAP: _____
_____
_____
_____
_____
_____

NIGHTLY GRATITUDE: _____
_____
_____
_____
_____
_____
_____

June 11

DAILY FOCUS: _____

DAILY COMMITMENT: _____
_____
_____

DAILY TOP TARGET: _____
_____
_____
_____

DAILY FOCUSED MEDITATION:

"I breathe in _____, I breathe out _____."

                DAILY GOALS: **DAILY FOCUS:**

_____   _____
_____   _____
_____   _____
_____   _____
_____   _____
_____   _____
_____   _____
_____   _____
_____   _____

NIGHTLY SUCCESS RECAP: _____
_____
_____
_____
_____
_____

NIGHTLY GRATITUDE:_____
_____
_____
_____
_____
_____
_____

DAILY FOCUS: _____

DAILY COMMITMENT: _____
_____
_____

DAILY TOP TARGET: _____
_____
_____
_____

DAILY FOCUSED MEDITATION:

"I breathe in _____, I breathe out _____."

DAILY GOALS:

_____
_____
_____
_____
_____
_____
_____
_____
_____

DAILY FOCUS:

_____
_____
_____
_____
_____
_____
_____
_____
_____

NIGHTLY SUCCESS RECAP: _____
_____
_____
_____
_____
_____
_____

NIGHTLY GRATITUDE: _____
_____
_____
_____
_____
_____
_____

June 13

DAILY FOCUS: _____

DAILY COMMITMENT: _____
_____
_____

DAILY TOP TARGET: _____
_____
_____
_____

DAILY FOCUSED MEDITATION:

"I breathe in _____, I breathe out _____."

DAILY GOALS:	DAILY FOCUS:
_____	_____
_____	_____
_____	_____
_____	_____
_____	_____
_____	_____
_____	_____
_____	_____
_____	_____

NIGHTLY SUCCESS RECAP: _____
_____
_____
_____
_____
_____
_____

NIGHTLY GRATITUDE: _____
_____
_____
_____
_____
_____
_____

DAILY FOCUS: _____

DAILY COMMITMENT: _____
_____
_____

DAILY TOP TARGET: _____
_____
_____
_____

DAILY FOCUSED MEDITATION:

"I breathe in _____, I breathe out _____."

DAILY GOALS:

_____
_____
_____
_____
_____
_____
_____
_____
_____
_____

DAILY FOCUS:

_____
_____
_____
_____
_____
_____
_____
_____
_____
_____

NIGHTLY SUCCESS RECAP: _____
_____
_____
_____
_____
_____
_____

NIGHTLY GRATITUDE: _____
_____
_____
_____
_____
_____
_____

June 15

DAILY FOCUS: _____

DAILY COMMITMENT: _____
_____
_____

DAILY TOP TARGET: _____
_____
_____
_____

DAILY FOCUSED MEDITATION:

"I breathe in _____, I breathe out _____."

DAILY GOALS: DAILY FOCUS:

_____	_____
_____	_____
_____	_____
_____	_____
_____	_____
_____	_____
_____	_____
_____	_____
_____	_____

NIGHTLY SUCCESS RECAP: _____
_____
_____
_____
_____
_____
_____

NIGHTLY GRATITUDE:_____
_____
_____
_____
_____
_____
_____

June 16

DAILY FOCUS: _____

DAILY COMMITMENT: _____
_____
_____

DAILY TOP TARGET: _____
_____
_____
_____

DAILY FOCUSED MEDITATION:

"I breathe in _____, I breathe out _____."

DAILY GOALS:

_____
_____
_____
_____
_____
_____
_____
_____
_____
_____

DAILY FOCUS:

_____
_____
_____
_____
_____
_____
_____
_____
_____
_____

NIGHTLY SUCCESS RECAP: _____
_____
_____
_____
_____
_____
_____

NIGHTLY GRATITUDE: _____
_____
_____
_____
_____
_____
_____

June 17

DAILY FOCUS: _____

DAILY COMMITMENT: _____
_____
_____

DAILY TOP TARGET: _____
_____
_____
_____

DAILY FOCUSED MEDITATION:

"I breathe in _____, I breathe out _____."

DAILY GOALS:	**DAILY FOCUS:**
_____	_____
_____	_____
_____	_____
_____	_____
_____	_____
_____	_____
_____	_____
_____	_____
_____	_____

NIGHTLY SUCCESS RECAP: _____
_____
_____
_____
_____
_____

NIGHTLY GRATITUDE:_____
_____
_____
_____
_____
_____

June 18

DAILY FOCUS: _____

DAILY COMMITMENT: _____
_____
_____

DAILY TOP TARGET: _____
_____
_____
_____

DAILY FOCUSED MEDITATION:

"I breathe in _____, I breathe out _____."

DAILY GOALS: **DAILY FOCUS:**

_____   _____
_____   _____
_____   _____
_____   _____
_____   _____
_____   _____
_____   _____
_____   _____
_____   _____

NIGHTLY SUCCESS RECAP: _____
_____
_____
_____
_____
_____
_____

NIGHTLY GRATITUDE: _____
_____
_____
_____
_____
_____
_____

June 19

DAILY FOCUS: _____

DAILY COMMITMENT: _____
_____
_____

DAILY TOP TARGET: _____
_____
_____
_____

DAILY FOCUSED MEDITATION:

"I breathe in _____, I breathe out _____."

DAILY GOALS:

_____
_____
_____
_____
_____
_____
_____
_____
_____
_____

DAILY FOCUS:

_____
_____
_____
_____
_____
_____
_____
_____
_____
_____

NIGHTLY SUCCESS RECAP: _____
_____
_____
_____
_____
_____
_____

NIGHTLY GRATITUDE: _____
_____
_____
_____
_____
_____
_____

DAILY FOCUS: _____

DAILY COMMITMENT: _____
_____
_____

DAILY TOP TARGET: _____
_____
_____
_____

DAILY FOCUSED MEDITATION:

"I breathe in _____, I breathe out _____."

DAILY GOALS:

_____
_____
_____
_____
_____
_____
_____
_____
_____
_____

DAILY FOCUS:

_____
_____
_____
_____
_____
_____
_____
_____
_____
_____

NIGHTLY SUCCESS RECAP: _____
_____
_____
_____
_____
_____
_____

NIGHTLY GRATITUDE:_____
_____
_____
_____
_____
_____
_____

June 21

DAILY FOCUS: _____

DAILY COMMITMENT: _____
_____
_____

DAILY TOP TARGET: _____
_____
_____
_____

DAILY FOCUSED MEDITATION:

"I breathe in _____, I breathe out _____."

DAILY GOALS:

_____
_____
_____
_____
_____
_____
_____
_____
_____

DAILY FOCUS:

_____
_____
_____
_____
_____
_____
_____
_____
_____

NIGHTLY SUCCESS RECAP: _____
_____
_____
_____
_____
_____

NIGHTLY GRATITUDE: _____
_____
_____
_____
_____
_____

June 22

DAILY FOCUS: _____

DAILY COMMITMENT: _____
_____
_____

DAILY TOP TARGET: _____
_____
_____
_____

DAILY FOCUSED MEDITATION:

"I breathe in _____, I breathe out _____."

DAILY GOALS:

_____
_____
_____
_____
_____
_____
_____
_____
_____
_____

DAILY FOCUS:

_____
_____
_____
_____
_____
_____
_____
_____
_____
_____

NIGHTLY SUCCESS RECAP: _____
_____
_____
_____
_____
_____
_____

NIGHTLY GRATITUDE: _____
_____
_____
_____
_____
_____
_____

June 23

DAILY FOCUS: _____

DAILY COMMITMENT: _____
_____
_____

DAILY TOP TARGET: _____
_____
_____
_____

DAILY FOCUSED MEDITATION:

"I breathe in _____, I breathe out _____."

DAILY GOALS:	**DAILY FOCUS:**
_____	_____
_____	_____
_____	_____
_____	_____
_____	_____
_____	_____
_____	_____
_____	_____
_____	_____

NIGHTLY SUCCESS RECAP: _____
_____
_____
_____
_____
_____

NIGHTLY GRATITUDE: _____
_____
_____
_____
_____
_____

DAILY FOCUS: _____

DAILY COMMITMENT: _____
_____
_____

DAILY TOP TARGET: _____
_____
_____
_____

DAILY FOCUSED MEDITATION:

"I breathe in _____, I breathe out _____."

DAILY GOALS:	**DAILY FOCUS:**
_____	_____
_____	_____
_____	_____
_____	_____
_____	_____
_____	_____
_____	_____
_____	_____
_____	_____

NIGHTLY SUCCESS RECAP: _____
_____
_____
_____
_____
_____

NIGHTLY GRATITUDE:_____
_____
_____
_____
_____
_____
_____

June 25

DAILY FOCUS: _____

DAILY COMMITMENT: _____
_____
_____

DAILY TOP TARGET: _____
_____
_____
_____

DAILY FOCUSED MEDITATION:

"I breathe in _____, I breathe out _____."

DAILY GOALS:	DAILY FOCUS:
_____	_____
_____	_____
_____	_____
_____	_____
_____	_____
_____	_____
_____	_____
_____	_____
_____	_____

NIGHTLY SUCCESS RECAP: _____
_____
_____
_____
_____
_____
_____

NIGHTLY GRATITUDE: _____
_____
_____
_____
_____
_____
_____

DAILY FOCUS: _____

DAILY COMMITMENT: _____
_____
_____

DAILY TOP TARGET: _____
_____
_____
_____

DAILY FOCUSED MEDITATION:

"I breathe in _____, I breathe out _____."

DAILY GOALS:

_____
_____
_____
_____
_____
_____
_____
_____
_____

DAILY FOCUS:

_____
_____
_____
_____
_____
_____
_____
_____
_____

NIGHTLY SUCCESS RECAP: _____
_____
_____
_____
_____
_____

NIGHTLY GRATITUDE: _____
_____
_____
_____
_____
_____

June 27

DAILY FOCUS: _____

DAILY COMMITMENT: _____
_____
_____

DAILY TOP TARGET: _____
_____
_____
_____

DAILY FOCUSED MEDITATION:

"I breathe in _____, I breathe out _____."

DAILY GOALS: DAILY FOCUS:

_____   _____
_____   _____
_____   _____
_____   _____
_____   _____
_____   _____
_____   _____
_____   _____
_____   _____

NIGHTLY SUCCESS RECAP: _____
_____
_____
_____
_____
_____
_____

NIGHTLY GRATITUDE:_____
_____
_____
_____
_____
_____
_____

DAILY FOCUS: _____

DAILY COMMITMENT: _____
_____
_____

DAILY TOP TARGET: _____
_____
_____
_____

DAILY FOCUSED MEDITATION:

"I breathe in _____, I breathe out _____."

DAILY GOALS: **DAILY FOCUS:**

_____   _____
_____   _____
_____   _____
_____   _____
_____   _____
_____   _____
_____   _____
_____   _____
_____   _____

NIGHTLY SUCCESS RECAP: _____
_____
_____
_____
_____
_____
_____

NIGHTLY GRATITUDE:_____
_____
_____
_____
_____
_____
_____

June 29

DAILY FOCUS: _____

DAILY COMMITMENT: _____
_____
_____

DAILY TOP TARGET: _____
_____
_____
_____

DAILY FOCUSED MEDITATION:

"I breathe in _____, I breathe out _____."

DAILY GOALS:	**DAILY FOCUS:**
_____	_____
_____	_____
_____	_____
_____	_____
_____	_____
_____	_____
_____	_____
_____	_____
_____	_____

NIGHTLY SUCCESS RECAP: _____
_____
_____
_____
_____
_____

NIGHTLY GRATITUDE: _____
_____
_____
_____
_____
_____

DAILY FOCUS: _____

DAILY COMMITMENT: _____
_____
_____

DAILY TOP TARGET: _____
_____
_____
_____

DAILY FOCUSED MEDITATION:

"I breathe in _____, I breathe out _____."

DAILY GOALS: **DAILY FOCUS:**

_____   _____
_____   _____
_____   _____
_____   _____
_____   _____
_____   _____
_____   _____
_____   _____

NIGHTLY SUCCESS RECAP: _____
_____
_____
_____
_____
_____
_____

NIGHTLY GRATITUDE:_____
_____
_____
_____
_____
_____
_____

July 1

DAILY FOCUS: _____

DAILY COMMITMENT: _____
_____
_____

DAILY TOP TARGET: _____
_____
_____
_____

DAILY FOCUSED MEDITATION:

"I breathe in _____, I breathe out _____."

DAILY GOALS:

_____
_____
_____
_____
_____
_____
_____
_____
_____

DAILY FOCUS:

_____
_____
_____
_____
_____
_____
_____
_____
_____

NIGHTLY SUCCESS RECAP: _____
_____
_____
_____
_____
_____
_____

NIGHTLY GRATITUDE: _____
_____
_____
_____
_____
_____
_____

DAILY FOCUS: _____

DAILY COMMITMENT: _____
_____
_____

DAILY TOP TARGET: _____
_____
_____
_____

DAILY FOCUSED MEDITATION:

"I breathe in _____, I breathe out _____."

DAILY GOALS: **DAILY FOCUS:**

_____	_____
_____	_____
_____	_____
_____	_____
_____	_____
_____	_____
_____	_____
_____	_____
_____	_____

NIGHTLY SUCCESS RECAP: _____
_____
_____
_____
_____
_____
_____

NIGHTLY GRATITUDE: _____
_____
_____
_____
_____
_____
_____

July 3

DAILY FOCUS: _____

DAILY COMMITMENT: _____
_____
_____

DAILY TOP TARGET: _____
_____
_____
_____

DAILY FOCUSED MEDITATION:

"I breathe in _____, I breathe out _____."

DAILY GOALS: **DAILY FOCUS:**

_____   _____
_____   _____
_____   _____
_____   _____
_____   _____
_____   _____
_____   _____
_____   _____
_____   _____

NIGHTLY SUCCESS RECAP: _____
_____
_____
_____
_____
_____

NIGHTLY GRATITUDE:_____
_____
_____
_____
_____
_____
_____

DAILY FOCUS: _____

DAILY COMMITMENT: _____
_____
_____

DAILY TOP TARGET: _____
_____
_____
_____

DAILY FOCUSED MEDITATION:

"I breathe in _____, I breathe out _____."

DAILY GOALS:

_____
_____
_____
_____
_____
_____
_____
_____
_____

DAILY FOCUS:

_____
_____
_____
_____
_____
_____
_____
_____
_____

NIGHTLY SUCCESS RECAP: _____
_____
_____
_____
_____
_____
_____

NIGHTLY GRATITUDE: _____
_____
_____
_____
_____
_____

July 5

DAILY FOCUS: _____

DAILY COMMITMENT: _____
_____
_____

DAILY TOP TARGET: _____
_____
_____
_____

DAILY FOCUSED MEDITATION:

"I breathe in _____, I breathe out _____."

DAILY GOALS: **DAILY FOCUS:**

_____   _____
_____   _____
_____   _____
_____   _____
_____   _____
_____   _____
_____   _____
_____   _____
_____   _____

NIGHTLY SUCCESS RECAP: _____
_____
_____
_____
_____
_____

NIGHTLY GRATITUDE: _____
_____
_____
_____
_____
_____

DAILY FOCUS: _____

DAILY COMMITMENT: _____
_____
_____

DAILY TOP TARGET: _____
_____
_____
_____

DAILY FOCUSED MEDITATION:

"I breathe in _____, I breathe out _____."

DAILY GOALS: **DAILY FOCUS:**

_____   _____
_____   _____
_____   _____
_____   _____
_____   _____
_____   _____
_____   _____
_____   _____
_____   _____

NIGHTLY SUCCESS RECAP: _____
_____
_____
_____
_____
_____

NIGHTLY GRATITUDE: _____
_____
_____
_____
_____
_____
_____

July 7

DAILY FOCUS: _____

DAILY COMMITMENT: _____
_____
_____

DAILY TOP TARGET: _____
_____
_____
_____

DAILY FOCUSED MEDITATION:

"I breathe in _____, I breathe out _____."

DAILY GOALS: **DAILY FOCUS:**

_____   _____
_____   _____
_____   _____
_____   _____
_____   _____
_____   _____
_____   _____
_____   _____
_____   _____

NIGHTLY SUCCESS RECAP: _____
_____
_____
_____
_____
_____

NIGHTLY GRATITUDE: _____
_____
_____
_____
_____
_____

DAILY FOCUS: _____

DAILY COMMITMENT: _____
_____
_____

DAILY TOP TARGET: _____
_____
_____
_____

DAILY FOCUSED MEDITATION:

"I breathe in _____, I breathe out _____."

DAILY GOALS:	**DAILY FOCUS:**
_____	_____
_____	_____
_____	_____
_____	_____
_____	_____
_____	_____
_____	_____
_____	_____
_____	_____

NIGHTLY SUCCESS RECAP: _____
_____
_____
_____
_____
_____

NIGHTLY GRATITUDE: _____
_____
_____
_____
_____
_____
_____

July 9

DAILY FOCUS: _____

DAILY COMMITMENT: _____
_____
_____

DAILY TOP TARGET: _____
_____
_____
_____

DAILY FOCUSED MEDITATION:

"I breathe in _____, I breathe out _____."

DAILY GOALS: **DAILY FOCUS:**

_____   _____
_____   _____
_____   _____
_____   _____
_____   _____
_____   _____
_____   _____
_____   _____
_____   _____

NIGHTLY SUCCESS RECAP: _____
_____
_____
_____
_____
_____

NIGHTLY GRATITUDE: _____
_____
_____
_____
_____
_____

July 10

DAILY FOCUS: _____

DAILY COMMITMENT: _____
_____
_____

DAILY TOP TARGET: _____
_____
_____
_____

DAILY FOCUSED MEDITATION:

"I breathe in _____, I breathe out _____."

<table>
<tr><td align="center">**DAILY GOALS:**</td><td align="center">**DAILY FOCUS:**</td></tr>
</table>

_____   _____
_____   _____
_____   _____
_____   _____
_____   _____
_____   _____
_____   _____
_____   _____
_____   _____

NIGHTLY SUCCESS RECAP: _____
_____
_____
_____
_____
_____

NIGHTLY GRATITUDE: _____
_____
_____
_____
_____
_____

July 11

DAILY FOCUS: _____

DAILY COMMITMENT: _____
_____
_____

DAILY TOP TARGET: _____
_____
_____
_____

DAILY FOCUSED MEDITATION:

"I breathe in _____, I breathe out _____."

<table>
<tr><td align="center">**DAILY GOALS:**</td><td align="center">**DAILY FOCUS:**</td></tr>
</table>

DAILY GOALS: **DAILY FOCUS:**

_____   _____
_____   _____
_____   _____
_____   _____
_____   _____
_____   _____
_____   _____
_____   _____
_____   _____

NIGHTLY SUCCESS RECAP: _____
_____
_____
_____
_____
_____

NIGHTLY GRATITUDE: _____
_____
_____
_____
_____
_____
_____

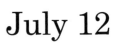

DAILY FOCUS: _____

DAILY COMMITMENT: _____
_____
_____

DAILY TOP TARGET: _____
_____
_____
_____

DAILY FOCUSED MEDITATION:

"I breathe in _____, I breathe out _____."

<table>
<tr><td align="center">**DAILY GOALS:**</td><td align="center">**DAILY FOCUS:**</td></tr>
</table>

DAILY GOALS:	DAILY FOCUS:
_____	_____
_____	_____
_____	_____
_____	_____
_____	_____
_____	_____
_____	_____
_____	_____
_____	_____

NIGHTLY SUCCESS RECAP: _____
_____
_____
_____
_____
_____

NIGHTLY GRATITUDE: _____
_____
_____
_____
_____
_____
_____

July 13

DAILY FOCUS: _____

DAILY COMMITMENT: _____
_____
_____

DAILY TOP TARGET: _____
_____
_____
_____

DAILY FOCUSED MEDITATION:

"I breathe in _____, I breathe out _____."

<table>
<tr><td align="center">DAILY GOALS:</td><td align="center">DAILY FOCUS:</td></tr>
</table>

_____	_____
_____	_____
_____	_____
_____	_____
_____	_____
_____	_____
_____	_____
_____	_____

NIGHTLY SUCCESS RECAP: _____
_____
_____
_____
_____
_____

NIGHTLY GRATITUDE: _____
_____
_____
_____
_____
_____

DAILY FOCUS: _____

DAILY COMMITMENT: _____
_____
_____

DAILY TOP TARGET: _____
_____
_____
_____

DAILY FOCUSED MEDITATION:

"I breathe in _____, I breathe out _____."

DAILY GOALS: **DAILY FOCUS:**

_____   _____
_____   _____
_____   _____
_____   _____
_____   _____
_____   _____
_____   _____
_____   _____
_____   _____

NIGHTLY SUCCESS RECAP: _____
_____
_____
_____
_____
_____
_____

NIGHTLY GRATITUDE: _____
_____
_____
_____
_____
_____
_____

July 15

DAILY FOCUS: _____

DAILY COMMITMENT: _____
_____
_____

DAILY TOP TARGET: _____
_____
_____
_____

DAILY FOCUSED MEDITATION:

"I breathe in _____, I breathe out _____."

DAILY GOALS:

_____
_____
_____
_____
_____
_____
_____
_____

DAILY FOCUS:

_____
_____
_____
_____
_____
_____
_____
_____

NIGHTLY SUCCESS RECAP: _____
_____
_____
_____
_____
_____

NIGHTLY GRATITUDE: _____
_____
_____
_____
_____
_____
_____

July 16

DAILY FOCUS: _____

DAILY COMMITMENT: _____
_____
_____

DAILY TOP TARGET: _____
_____
_____
_____

DAILY FOCUSED MEDITATION:

"I breathe in _____, I breathe out _____."

DAILY GOALS: DAILY FOCUS:

_____   _____
_____   _____
_____   _____
_____   _____
_____   _____
_____   _____
_____   _____
_____   _____
_____   _____

NIGHTLY SUCCESS RECAP: _____
_____
_____
_____
_____
_____

NIGHTLY GRATITUDE: _____
_____
_____
_____
_____
_____
_____

July 17

DAILY FOCUS: _____

DAILY COMMITMENT: _____
_____
_____

DAILY TOP TARGET: _____
_____
_____
_____

DAILY FOCUSED MEDITATION:

"I breathe in _____, I breathe out _____."

DAILY GOALS:	DAILY FOCUS:
_____	_____
_____	_____
_____	_____
_____	_____
_____	_____
_____	_____
_____	_____
_____	_____
_____	_____
_____	_____

NIGHTLY SUCCESS RECAP: _____
_____
_____
_____
_____
_____
_____

NIGHTLY GRATITUDE: _____
_____
_____
_____
_____
_____
_____

DAILY FOCUS: _____

DAILY COMMITMENT: _____
_____
_____

DAILY TOP TARGET: _____
_____
_____
_____

DAILY FOCUSED MEDITATION:

"I breathe in _____, I breathe out _____."

<table>
<tr><td align="center">DAILY GOALS:</td><td align="center">DAILY FOCUS:</td></tr>
</table>

DAILY GOALS: DAILY FOCUS:

_____   _____
_____   _____
_____   _____
_____   _____
_____   _____
_____   _____
_____   _____
_____   _____
_____   _____

NIGHTLY SUCCESS RECAP; _____
_____
_____
_____
_____

NIGHTLY GRATITUDE:_____
_____
_____
_____
_____
_____

July 19

DAILY FOCUS: _____

DAILY COMMITMENT: _____
_____
_____

DAILY TOP TARGET: _____
_____
_____
_____

DAILY FOCUSED MEDITATION:

"I breathe in _____, I breathe out _____."

DAILY GOALS: **DAILY FOCUS:**

_____   _____
_____   _____
_____   _____
_____   _____
_____   _____
_____   _____
_____   _____
_____   _____
_____   _____

NIGHTLY SUCCESS RECAP: _____
_____
_____
_____
_____
_____

NIGHTLY GRATITUDE: _____
_____
_____
_____
_____
_____
_____

DAILY FOCUS: _____

DAILY COMMITMENT: _____
_____
_____

DAILY TOP TARGET: _____
_____
_____
_____

DAILY FOCUSED MEDITATION:

"I breathe in _____, I breathe out _____."

<table>
<tr><td align="center">**DAILY GOALS:**</td><td align="center">**DAILY FOCUS:**</td></tr>
</table>

DAILY GOALS:	DAILY FOCUS:
_____	_____
_____	_____
_____	_____
_____	_____
_____	_____
_____	_____
_____	_____
_____	_____
_____	_____

NIGHTLY SUCCESS RECAP: _____
_____
_____
_____
_____
_____

NIGHTLY GRATITUDE: _____
_____
_____
_____
_____
_____
_____

July 21

DAILY FOCUS: _____

DAILY COMMITMENT: _____
_____
_____

DAILY TOP TARGET: _____
_____
_____
_____

DAILY FOCUSED MEDITATION:

"I breathe in _____, I breathe out _____."

DAILY GOALS:

_____
_____
_____
_____
_____
_____
_____
_____
_____

DAILY FOCUS:

_____
_____
_____
_____
_____
_____
_____
_____
_____

NIGHTLY SUCCESS RECAP: _____
_____
_____
_____
_____
_____

NIGHTLY GRATITUDE: _____
_____
_____
_____
_____
_____
_____

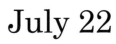
July 22

DAILY FOCUS: _____

DAILY COMMITMENT: _____
_____
_____

DAILY TOP TARGET: _____
_____
_____
_____

DAILY FOCUSED MEDITATION:

"I breathe in _____, I breathe out _____."

DAILY GOALS: **DAILY FOCUS:**

_____   _____
_____   _____
_____   _____
_____   _____
_____   _____
_____   _____
_____   _____
_____   _____
_____   _____

NIGHTLY SUCCESS RECAP: _____
_____
_____
_____
_____
_____

NIGHTLY GRATITUDE: _____
_____
_____
_____
_____
_____

July 23

DAILY FOCUS: _____

DAILY COMMITMENT: _____
_____
_____

DAILY TOP TARGET: _____
_____
_____
_____

DAILY FOCUSED MEDITATION:

"I breathe in _____, I breathe out _____."

DAILY GOALS:	**DAILY FOCUS:**
_____	_____
_____	_____
_____	_____
_____	_____
_____	_____
_____	_____
_____	_____
_____	_____
_____	_____

NIGHTLY SUCCESS RECAP: _____
_____
_____
_____
_____
_____

NIGHTLY GRATITUDE:_____
_____
_____
_____
_____
_____
_____

DAILY FOCUS: _____

DAILY COMMITMENT: _____
_____
_____

DAILY TOP TARGET: _____
_____
_____
_____

DAILY FOCUSED MEDITATION:

"I breathe in _____, I breathe out _____."

<table>
<tr><td align="center">DAILY GOALS:</td><td align="center">DAILY FOCUS:</td></tr>
</table>

NIGHTLY SUCCESS RECAP: _____
_____
_____
_____
_____
_____

NIGHTLY GRATITUDE: _____
_____
_____
_____
_____
_____

July 25

DAILY FOCUS: _____

DAILY COMMITMENT: _____
_____
_____

DAILY TOP TARGET: _____
_____
_____
_____

DAILY FOCUSED MEDITATION:

"I breathe in _____, I breathe out _____."

DAILY GOALS:	**DAILY FOCUS:**
_____	_____
_____	_____
_____	_____
_____	_____
_____	_____
_____	_____
_____	_____
_____	_____
_____	_____

NIGHTLY SUCCESS RECAP: _____
_____
_____
_____
_____
_____

NIGHTLY GRATITUDE: _____
_____
_____
_____
_____
_____
_____

DAILY FOCUS: _____

DAILY COMMITMENT: _____
_____
_____

DAILY TOP TARGET: _____
_____
_____
_____

DAILY FOCUSED MEDITATION:

"I breathe in _____, I breathe out _____."

DAILY GOALS:

_____
_____
_____
_____
_____
_____
_____
_____
_____
_____

DAILY FOCUS:

_____
_____
_____
_____
_____
_____
_____
_____
_____
_____

NIGHTLY SUCCESS RECAP: _____
_____
_____
_____
_____
_____

NIGHTLY GRATITUDE: _____
_____
_____
_____
_____
_____

July 27

DAILY FOCUS: _____

DAILY COMMITMENT: _____
_____
_____

DAILY TOP TARGET: _____
_____
_____
_____

DAILY FOCUSED MEDITATION:

"I breathe in _____, I breathe out _____."

DAILY GOALS:	DAILY FOCUS:
_____	_____
_____	_____
_____	_____
_____	_____
_____	_____
_____	_____
_____	_____
_____	_____
_____	_____

NIGHTLY SUCCESS RECAP: _____
_____
_____
_____
_____
_____

NIGHTLY GRATITUDE: _____
_____
_____
_____
_____
_____
_____

DAILY FOCUS: _____

DAILY COMMITMENT: _____
_____
_____

DAILY TOP TARGET: _____
_____
_____
_____

DAILY FOCUSED MEDITATION:

"I breathe in _____**, I breathe out** _____**."**

DAILY GOALS:

_____
_____
_____
_____
_____
_____
_____
_____
_____
_____

DAILY FOCUS:

_____
_____
_____
_____
_____
_____
_____
_____
_____
_____

NIGHTLY SUCCESS RECAP: _____
_____
_____
_____
_____
_____

NIGHTLY GRATITUDE: _____
_____
_____
_____
_____
_____
_____

July 29

DAILY FOCUS: _____

DAILY COMMITMENT: _____
_____
_____

DAILY TOP TARGET: _____
_____
_____
_____

DAILY FOCUSED MEDITATION:

"I breathe in _____, I breathe out _____."

DAILY GOALS:	**DAILY FOCUS:**
_____	_____
_____	_____
_____	_____
_____	_____
_____	_____
_____	_____
_____	_____
_____	_____
_____	_____

NIGHTLY SUCCESS RECAP: _____
_____
_____
_____
_____
_____

NIGHTLY GRATITUDE: _____
_____
_____
_____
_____
_____
_____

DAILY FOCUS: _____

DAILY COMMITMENT: _____
_____
_____

DAILY TOP TARGET: _____
_____
_____
_____

DAILY FOCUSED MEDITATION:

"I breathe in _____, I breathe out _____."

                    DAILY GOALS: **DAILY FOCUS:**

_____   _____
_____   _____
_____   _____
_____   _____
_____   _____
_____   _____
_____   _____
_____   _____
_____   _____

NIGHTLY SUCCESS RECAP: _____
_____
_____
_____
_____
_____

NIGHTLY GRATITUDE: _____
_____
_____
_____
_____
_____

July 31

DAILY FOCUS: _____

DAILY COMMITMENT: _____
_____
_____

DAILY TOP TARGET: _____
_____
_____
_____

DAILY FOCUSED MEDITATION:

"I breathe in _____, I breathe out _____."

DAILY GOALS:	**DAILY FOCUS:**
_____	_____
_____	_____
_____	_____
_____	_____
_____	_____
_____	_____
_____	_____
_____	_____
_____	_____

NIGHTLY SUCCESS RECAP: _____
_____
_____
_____
_____
_____

NIGHTLY GRATITUDE: _____
_____
_____
_____
_____
_____
_____

August 1

DAILY FOCUS: _____

DAILY COMMITMENT: _____
_____
_____

DAILY TOP TARGET: _____
_____
_____
_____

DAILY FOCUSED MEDITATION:

"I breathe in _____, I breathe out _____."

DAILY GOALS: **DAILY FOCUS:**

_____   _____
_____   _____
_____   _____
_____   _____
_____   _____
_____   _____
_____   _____
_____   _____
_____   _____

NIGHTLY SUCCESS RECAP: _____
_____
_____
_____
_____
_____

NIGHTLY GRATITUDE:_____
_____
_____
_____
_____
_____
_____

August 2

DAILY FOCUS: _____

DAILY COMMITMENT: _____
_____
_____

DAILY TOP TARGET: _____
_____
_____
_____

DAILY FOCUSED MEDITATION:

"I breathe in _____, I breathe out _____."

DAILY GOALS:	DAILY FOCUS:
_____	_____
_____	_____
_____	_____
_____	_____
_____	_____
_____	_____
_____	_____
_____	_____
_____	_____

NIGHTLY SUCCESS RECAP: _____
_____
_____
_____
_____
_____

NIGHTLY GRATITUDE:_____
_____
_____
_____
_____
_____
_____

August 3

DAILY FOCUS: _____

DAILY COMMITMENT: _____
_____
_____

DAILY TOP TARGET: _____
_____
_____
_____

DAILY FOCUSED MEDITATION:

"I breathe in _____, I breathe out _____."

DAILY GOALS:

_____
_____
_____
_____
_____
_____
_____
_____
_____

DAILY FOCUS:

_____
_____
_____
_____
_____
_____
_____
_____
_____

NIGHTLY SUCCESS RECAP: _____
_____
_____
_____
_____
_____

NIGHTLY GRATITUDE:_____
_____
_____
_____
_____
_____
_____

August 4

DAILY FOCUS: _____

DAILY COMMITMENT: _____
_____
_____

DAILY TOP TARGET: _____
_____
_____
_____

DAILY FOCUSED MEDITATION:

"I breathe in _____, I breathe out _____."

DAILY GOALS:

_____
_____
_____
_____
_____
_____
_____
_____
_____

DAILY FOCUS:

_____
_____
_____
_____
_____
_____
_____
_____
_____

NIGHTLY SUCCESS RECAP: _____
_____
_____
_____
_____
_____

NIGHTLY GRATITUDE: _____
_____
_____
_____
_____
_____
_____

August 5

DAILY FOCUS: _____

DAILY COMMITMENT: _____
_____
_____

DAILY TOP TARGET: _____
_____
_____
_____

DAILY FOCUSED MEDITATION:

"I breathe in _____, I breathe out _____."

DAILY GOALS:	**DAILY FOCUS:**
_____	_____
_____	_____
_____	_____
_____	_____
_____	_____
_____	_____
_____	_____
_____	_____
_____	_____

NIGHTLY SUCCESS RECAP: _____
_____
_____
_____
_____
_____

NIGHTLY GRATITUDE: _____
_____
_____
_____
_____
_____

August 6

DAILY FOCUS: _____

DAILY COMMITMENT: _____
_____
_____

DAILY TOP TARGET: _____
_____
_____
_____

DAILY FOCUSED MEDITATION:

"I breathe in _____, I breathe out _____."

DAILY GOALS:	**DAILY FOCUS:**
_____	_____
_____	_____
_____	_____
_____	_____
_____	_____
_____	_____
_____	_____
_____	_____
_____	_____

NIGHTLY SUCCESS RECAP: _____
_____
_____
_____
_____
_____

NIGHTLY GRATITUDE: _____
_____
_____
_____
_____
_____

August 7

DAILY FOCUS: _____

DAILY COMMITMENT: _____
_____
_____

DAILY TOP TARGET: _____
_____
_____
_____

DAILY FOCUSED MEDITATION:

"I breathe in _____, I breathe out _____."

DAILY GOALS:	**DAILY FOCUS:**
_____	_____
_____	_____
_____	_____
_____	_____
_____	_____
_____	_____
_____	_____
_____	_____

NIGHTLY SUCCESS RECAP: _____
_____
_____
_____
_____
_____

NIGHTLY GRATITUDE: _____
_____
_____
_____
_____
_____

August 8

DAILY FOCUS: _____

DAILY COMMITMENT: _____
_____
_____

DAILY TOP TARGET: _____
_____
_____
_____

DAILY FOCUSED MEDITATION:

"I breathe in _____, I breathe out _____."

DAILY GOALS: **DAILY FOCUS:**

_____   _____
_____   _____
_____   _____
_____   _____
_____   _____
_____   _____
_____   _____
_____   _____
_____   _____

NIGHTLY SUCCESS RECAP: _____
_____
_____
_____
_____
_____

NIGHTLY GRATITUDE: _____
_____
_____
_____
_____
_____

DAILY FOCUS: _____

DAILY COMMITMENT: _____
_____
_____

DAILY TOP TARGET: _____
_____
_____
_____

DAILY FOCUSED MEDITATION:

"I breathe in _____, I breathe out _____."

DAILY GOALS:

_____
_____
_____
_____
_____
_____
_____
_____
_____
_____

DAILY FOCUS:

_____
_____
_____
_____
_____
_____
_____
_____
_____
_____

NIGHTLY SUCCESS RECAP: _____
_____
_____
_____
_____
_____
_____

NIGHTLY GRATITUDE: _____
_____
_____
_____
_____
_____
_____

August 10

DAILY FOCUS: _____

DAILY COMMITMENT: _____
_____
_____

DAILY TOP TARGET: _____
_____
_____
_____

DAILY FOCUSED MEDITATION:

"I breathe in _____, I breathe out _____."

DAILY GOALS: **DAILY FOCUS:**

_____   _____
_____   _____
_____   _____
_____   _____
_____   _____
_____   _____
_____   _____
_____   _____
_____   _____

NIGHTLY SUCCESS RECAP: _____
_____
_____
_____
_____
_____

NIGHTLY GRATITUDE: _____
_____
_____
_____
_____
_____

DAILY FOCUS: _____

DAILY COMMITMENT: _____
_____
_____

DAILY TOP TARGET: _____
_____
_____
_____

DAILY FOCUSED MEDITATION:

"I breathe in _____, I breathe out _____."

DAILY GOALS: **DAILY FOCUS:**

_____   _____
_____   _____
_____   _____
_____   _____
_____   _____
_____   _____
_____   _____
_____   _____
_____   _____
_____   _____

NIGHTLY SUCCESS RECAP: _____
_____
_____
_____
_____
_____

NIGHTLY GRATITUDE: _____
_____
_____
_____
_____
_____

August 12

DAILY FOCUS: _____

DAILY COMMITMENT: _____
_____
_____

DAILY TOP TARGET: _____
_____
_____
_____

DAILY FOCUSED MEDITATION:

"I breathe in _____, I breathe out _____."

DAILY GOALS:	**DAILY FOCUS:**
_____	_____
_____	_____
_____	_____
_____	_____
_____	_____
_____	_____
_____	_____
_____	_____
_____	_____

NIGHTLY SUCCESS RECAP: _____
_____
_____
_____
_____
_____

NIGHTLY GRATITUDE: _____
_____
_____
_____
_____
_____

DAILY FOCUS: _____

DAILY COMMITMENT: _____
_____
_____

DAILY TOP TARGET: _____
_____
_____
_____

DAILY FOCUSED MEDITATION:

"I breathe in _____, I breathe out _____."

DAILY GOALS:	**DAILY FOCUS:**
_____	_____
_____	_____
_____	_____
_____	_____
_____	_____
_____	_____
_____	_____
_____	_____
_____	_____

NIGHTLY SUCCESS RECAP: _____
_____
_____
_____
_____
_____

NIGHTLY GRATITUDE: _____
_____
_____
_____
_____
_____

August 14

DAILY FOCUS: _____

DAILY COMMITMENT: _____
_____
_____

DAILY TOP TARGET: _____
_____
_____
_____

DAILY FOCUSED MEDITATION:

"I breathe in _____, I breathe out _____."

DAILY GOALS: **DAILY FOCUS:**

_____   _____
_____   _____
_____   _____
_____   _____
_____   _____
_____   _____
_____   _____
_____   _____
_____   _____
_____   _____

NIGHTLY SUCCESS RECAP: _____
_____
_____
_____
_____
_____
_____

NIGHTLY GRATITUDE: _____
_____
_____
_____
_____
_____
_____

August 15

DAILY FOCUS: _____

DAILY COMMITMENT: _____
_____
_____

DAILY TOP TARGET: _____
_____
_____
_____

DAILY FOCUSED MEDITATION:

"I breathe in _____, I breathe out _____."

DAILY GOALS:	**DAILY FOCUS:**
_____	_____
_____	_____
_____	_____
_____	_____
_____	_____
_____	_____
_____	_____
_____	_____
_____	_____

NIGHTLY SUCCESS RECAP: _____
_____
_____
_____
_____
_____

NIGHTLY GRATITUDE:_____
_____
_____
_____
_____
_____

August 16

DAILY FOCUS: _____

DAILY COMMITMENT: _____
_____
_____

DAILY TOP TARGET: _____
_____
_____
_____

DAILY FOCUSED MEDITATION:

"I breathe in _____, I breathe out _____."

DAILY GOALS:

_____
_____
_____
_____
_____
_____
_____
_____
_____

DAILY FOCUS:

_____
_____
_____
_____
_____
_____
_____
_____
_____

NIGHTLY SUCCESS RECAP: _____
_____
_____
_____
_____
_____

NIGHTLY GRATITUDE:_____
_____
_____
_____
_____
_____
_____

DAILY FOCUS: _____

DAILY COMMITMENT: _____
_____
_____

DAILY TOP TARGET: _____
_____
_____
_____

DAILY FOCUSED MEDITATION:

"I breathe in _____, I breathe out _____."

DAILY GOALS:	**DAILY FOCUS:**
_____	_____
_____	_____
_____	_____
_____	_____
_____	_____
_____	_____
_____	_____
_____	_____
_____	_____

NIGHTLY SUCCESS RECAP: _____
_____
_____
_____
_____
_____

NIGHTLY GRATITUDE: _____
_____
_____
_____
_____
_____
_____

August 18

DAILY FOCUS: _____

DAILY COMMITMENT: _____
_____
_____

DAILY TOP TARGET: _____
_____
_____
_____

DAILY FOCUSED MEDITATION:

"I breathe in _____, I breathe out _____."

DAILY GOALS:	**DAILY FOCUS:**
_____	_____
_____	_____
_____	_____
_____	_____
_____	_____
_____	_____
_____	_____
_____	_____
_____	_____

NIGHTLY SUCCESS RECAP: _____
_____
_____
_____
_____
_____

NIGHTLY GRATITUDE: _____
_____
_____
_____
_____
_____
_____

DAILY FOCUS: _____

DAILY COMMITMENT: _____
_____
_____

DAILY TOP TARGET: _____
_____
_____
_____

DAILY FOCUSED MEDITATION:

"I breathe in _____, I breathe out _____."

DAILY GOALS: **DAILY FOCUS:**

_____   _____
_____   _____
_____   _____
_____   _____
_____   _____
_____   _____
_____   _____
_____   _____
_____   _____

NIGHTLY SUCCESS RECAP: _____
_____
_____
_____
_____
_____
_____

NIGHTLY GRATITUDE: _____
_____
_____
_____
_____
_____

August 20

DAILY FOCUS: _____

DAILY COMMITMENT: _____
_____
_____

DAILY TOP TARGET: _____
_____
_____
_____

DAILY FOCUSED MEDITATION:

"I breathe in _____, I breathe out _____."

DAILY GOALS:	DAILY FOCUS:
_____	_____
_____	_____
_____	_____
_____	_____
_____	_____
_____	_____
_____	_____
_____	_____

NIGHTLY SUCCESS RECAP: _____
_____
_____
_____
_____
_____

NIGHTLY GRATITUDE:_____
_____
_____
_____
_____
_____
_____

August 21

DAILY FOCUS: _____

DAILY COMMITMENT: _____
_____
_____

DAILY TOP TARGET: _____
_____
_____
_____

DAILY FOCUSED MEDITATION:

"I breathe in _____, I breathe out _____."

DAILY GOALS:	**DAILY FOCUS:**
_____	_____
_____	_____
_____	_____
_____	_____
_____	_____
_____	_____
_____	_____
_____	_____
_____	_____

NIGHTLY SUCCESS RECAP: _____
_____
_____
_____
_____
_____

NIGHTLY GRATITUDE: _____
_____
_____
_____
_____
_____

August 22

DAILY FOCUS: _____

DAILY COMMITMENT: _____
_____
_____

DAILY TOP TARGET: _____
_____
_____
_____

DAILY FOCUSED MEDITATION:

"I breathe in _____, I breathe out _____."

DAILY GOALS:	DAILY FOCUS:
_____	_____
_____	_____
_____	_____
_____	_____
_____	_____
_____	_____
_____	_____
_____	_____
_____	_____

NIGHTLY SUCCESS RECAP: _____
_____
_____
_____
_____
_____

NIGHTLY GRATITUDE:_____
_____
_____
_____
_____
_____
_____

August 23

DAILY FOCUS: _____

DAILY COMMITMENT: _____
_____
_____

DAILY TOP TARGET: _____
_____
_____
_____

DAILY FOCUSED MEDITATION:

"I breathe in _____, I breathe out _____."

DAILY GOALS:

DAILY FOCUS:

_____   _____
_____   _____
_____   _____
_____   _____
_____   _____
_____   _____
_____   _____
_____   _____
_____   _____

NIGHTLY SUCCESS RECAP: _____
_____
_____
_____
_____
_____
_____

NIGHTLY GRATITUDE:_____
_____
_____
_____
_____
_____

August 24

DAILY FOCUS: _____

DAILY COMMITMENT: _____
_____
_____

DAILY TOP TARGET: _____
_____
_____
_____

DAILY FOCUSED MEDITATION:

"I breathe in _____, I breathe out _____."

DAILY GOALS: **DAILY FOCUS:**

_____   _____
_____   _____
_____   _____
_____   _____
_____   _____
_____   _____
_____   _____
_____   _____
_____   _____

NIGHTLY SUCCESS RECAP: _____
_____
_____
_____
_____

NIGHTLY GRATITUDE:_____
_____
_____
_____
_____
_____
_____

DAILY FOCUS: _____

DAILY COMMITMENT: _____
_____
_____

DAILY TOP TARGET: _____
_____
_____
_____

DAILY FOCUSED MEDITATION:

"I breathe in _____, I breathe out _____."

DAILY GOALS:	**DAILY FOCUS:**
_____	_____
_____	_____
_____	_____
_____	_____
_____	_____
_____	_____
_____	_____
_____	_____
_____	_____

NIGHTLY SUCCESS RECAP: _____
_____
_____
_____
_____
_____

NIGHTLY GRATITUDE:_____
_____
_____
_____
_____
_____

August 26

DAILY FOCUS: _____

DAILY COMMITMENT: _____
_____
_____

DAILY TOP TARGET: _____
_____
_____
_____

DAILY FOCUSED MEDITATION:

"I breathe in _____, I breathe out _____."

DAILY GOALS:

_____
_____
_____
_____
_____
_____
_____
_____
_____

DAILY FOCUS:

_____
_____
_____
_____
_____
_____
_____
_____
_____

NIGHTLY SUCCESS RECAP: _____
_____
_____
_____
_____
_____

NIGHTLY GRATITUDE:_____
_____
_____
_____
_____
_____
_____

August 27

DAILY FOCUS: _____

DAILY COMMITMENT: _____
_____
_____

DAILY TOP TARGET: _____
_____
_____
_____

DAILY FOCUSED MEDITATION:

"I breathe in _____, I breathe out _____."

DAILY GOALS:	DAILY FOCUS:
_____	_____
_____	_____
_____	_____
_____	_____
_____	_____
_____	_____
_____	_____
_____	_____
_____	_____

NIGHTLY SUCCESS RECAP: _____
_____
_____
_____
_____
_____

NIGHTLY GRATITUDE: _____
_____
_____
_____
_____
_____

August 28

DAILY FOCUS: _____

DAILY COMMITMENT: _____
_____
_____

DAILY TOP TARGET: _____
_____
_____
_____

DAILY FOCUSED MEDITATION:

"I breathe in _____, I breathe out _____."

DAILY GOALS:	**DAILY FOCUS:**
_____	_____
_____	_____
_____	_____
_____	_____
_____	_____
_____	_____
_____	_____
_____	_____
_____	_____
_____	_____

NIGHTLY SUCCESS RECAP: _____
_____
_____
_____
_____
_____

NIGHTLY GRATITUDE: _____
_____
_____
_____
_____
_____

DAILY FOCUS: _____

DAILY COMMITMENT: _____
_____
_____

DAILY TOP TARGET: _____
_____
_____
_____

DAILY FOCUSED MEDITATION:

"I breathe in _____, I breathe out _____."

DAILY GOALS:

_____
_____
_____
_____
_____
_____
_____
_____
_____
_____

DAILY FOCUS:

_____
_____
_____
_____
_____
_____
_____
_____
_____
_____

NIGHTLY SUCCESS RECAP: _____
_____
_____
_____
_____
_____
_____

NIGHTLY GRATITUDE: _____
_____
_____
_____
_____
_____
_____

August 30

DAILY FOCUS: _____

DAILY COMMITMENT: _____
_____
_____

DAILY TOP TARGET: _____
_____
_____
_____

DAILY FOCUSED MEDITATION:

"I breathe in _____, I breathe out _____."

DAILY GOALS:	**DAILY FOCUS:**
_____	_____
_____	_____
_____	_____
_____	_____
_____	_____
_____	_____
_____	_____
_____	_____
_____	_____

NIGHTLY SUCCESS RECAP: _____
_____
_____
_____
_____
_____

NIGHTLY GRATITUDE: _____
_____
_____
_____
_____
_____
_____

DAILY FOCUS: _____

DAILY COMMITMENT: _____
_____
_____

DAILY TOP TARGET: _____
_____
_____
_____

DAILY FOCUSED MEDITATION:

"I breathe in _____, I breathe out _____."

DAILY GOALS: **DAILY FOCUS:**

_____   _____
_____   _____
_____   _____
_____   _____
_____   _____
_____   _____
_____   _____
_____   _____
_____   _____

NIGHTLY SUCCESS RECAP: _____
_____
_____
_____
_____
_____
_____

NIGHTLY GRATITUDE: _____
_____
_____
_____
_____
_____

September 1

DAILY FOCUS: _____

DAILY COMMITMENT: _____
_____
_____

DAILY TOP TARGET: _____
_____
_____
_____

DAILY FOCUSED MEDITATION:

"I breathe in _____, I breathe out _____."

DAILY GOALS:	**DAILY FOCUS:**
_____	_____
_____	_____
_____	_____
_____	_____
_____	_____
_____	_____
_____	_____
_____	_____

NIGHTLY SUCCESS RECAP: _____
_____
_____
_____
_____
_____

NIGHTLY GRATITUDE: _____
_____
_____
_____
_____
_____
_____

September 2

DAILY FOCUS: _____

DAILY COMMITMENT: _____
_____
_____

DAILY TOP TARGET: _____
_____
_____
_____

DAILY FOCUSED MEDITATION:

"I breathe in _____, I breathe out _____."

DAILY GOALS:

_____
_____
_____
_____
_____
_____
_____
_____

DAILY FOCUS:

_____
_____
_____
_____
_____
_____
_____
_____

NIGHTLY SUCCESS RECAP: _____
_____
_____
_____
_____
_____

NIGHTLY GRATITUDE: _____
_____
_____
_____
_____
_____

September 3

DAILY FOCUS: _____

DAILY COMMITMENT: _____
_____
_____

DAILY TOP TARGET: _____
_____
_____
_____

DAILY FOCUSED MEDITATION:

"I breathe in _____, I breathe out _____."

DAILY GOALS:	**DAILY FOCUS:**
_____	_____
_____	_____
_____	_____
_____	_____
_____	_____
_____	_____
_____	_____
_____	_____

NIGHTLY SUCCESS RECAP: _____
_____
_____
_____
_____
_____

NIGHTLY GRATITUDE: _____
_____
_____
_____
_____
_____
_____

September 4

DAILY FOCUS: _____

DAILY COMMITMENT: _____
_____
_____

DAILY TOP TARGET: _____
_____
_____
_____

DAILY FOCUSED MEDITATION:

"I breathe in _____, I breathe out _____."

DAILY GOALS: **DAILY FOCUS:**

_____   _____
_____   _____
_____   _____
_____   _____
_____   _____
_____   _____
_____   _____
_____   _____
_____   _____

NIGHTLY SUCCESS RECAP: _____
_____
_____
_____
_____
_____

NIGHTLY GRATITUDE:_____
_____
_____
_____
_____
_____

September 5

DAILY FOCUS: _____

DAILY COMMITMENT: _____
_____
_____

DAILY TOP TARGET: _____
_____
_____
_____

DAILY FOCUSED MEDITATION:

"I breathe in _____, I breathe out _____."

DAILY GOALS:	DAILY FOCUS:
_____	_____
_____	_____
_____	_____
_____	_____
_____	_____
_____	_____
_____	_____
_____	_____
_____	_____

NIGHTLY SUCCESS RECAP: _____
_____
_____
_____
_____
_____
_____

NIGHTLY GRATITUDE: _____
_____
_____
_____
_____
_____
_____

September 6

DAILY FOCUS: _____

DAILY COMMITMENT: _____
_____
_____

DAILY TOP TARGET: _____
_____
_____
_____

DAILY FOCUSED MEDITATION:

"I breathe in _____, I breathe out _____."

DAILY GOALS:	DAILY FOCUS:
_____	_____
_____	_____
_____	_____
_____	_____
_____	_____
_____	_____
_____	_____
_____	_____
_____	_____

NIGHTLY SUCCESS RECAP: _____
_____
_____
_____
_____
_____

NIGHTLY GRATITUDE: _____
_____
_____
_____
_____
_____

September 7

DAILY FOCUS: _____

DAILY COMMITMENT: _____
_____
_____

DAILY TOP TARGET: _____
_____
_____
_____

DAILY FOCUSED MEDITATION:

"I breathe in _____, I breathe out _____."

DAILY GOALS:	**DAILY FOCUS:**
_____	_____
_____	_____
_____	_____
_____	_____
_____	_____
_____	_____
_____	_____
_____	_____
_____	_____

NIGHTLY SUCCESS RECAP: _____
_____
_____
_____
_____
_____

NIGHTLY GRATITUDE: _____
_____
_____
_____
_____
_____
_____

September 8

DAILY FOCUS: _____

DAILY COMMITMENT: _____
_____
_____

DAILY TOP TARGET: _____
_____
_____
_____

DAILY FOCUSED MEDITATION:

"I breathe in _____, I breathe out _____."

DAILY GOALS: **DAILY FOCUS:**

_____   _____
_____   _____
_____   _____
_____   _____
_____   _____
_____   _____
_____   _____
_____   _____
_____   _____

NIGHTLY SUCCESS RECAP: _____
_____
_____
_____
_____
_____

NIGHTLY GRATITUDE: _____
_____
_____
_____
_____
_____
_____

September 9

DAILY FOCUS: _____

DAILY COMMITMENT: _____
_____
_____

DAILY TOP TARGET: _____
_____
_____
_____

DAILY FOCUSED MEDITATION:

"I breathe in _____, I breathe out _____."

DAILY GOALS:	**DAILY FOCUS:**
_____	_____
_____	_____
_____	_____
_____	_____
_____	_____
_____	_____
_____	_____
_____	_____
_____	_____

NIGHTLY SUCCESS RECAP: _____
_____
_____
_____
_____
_____

NIGHTLY GRATITUDE: _____
_____
_____
_____
_____
_____
_____

September 10

DAILY FOCUS: _____

DAILY COMMITMENT: _____
_____
_____

DAILY TOP TARGET: _____
_____
_____
_____

DAILY FOCUSED MEDITATION:

"I breathe in _____, I breathe out _____."

DAILY GOALS:

_____
_____
_____
_____
_____
_____
_____
_____
_____
_____

DAILY FOCUS:

_____
_____
_____
_____
_____
_____
_____
_____
_____
_____

NIGHTLY SUCCESS RECAP: _____
_____
_____
_____
_____
_____

NIGHTLY GRATITUDE: _____
_____
_____
_____
_____
_____
_____

September 11

DAILY FOCUS: _____

DAILY COMMITMENT: _____
_____
_____

DAILY TOP TARGET: _____
_____
_____
_____

DAILY FOCUSED MEDITATION:

"I breathe in _____, I breathe out _____."

DAILY GOALS:

_____
_____
_____
_____
_____
_____
_____
_____
_____

DAILY FOCUS:

_____
_____
_____
_____
_____
_____
_____
_____
_____

NIGHTLY SUCCESS RECAP: _____
_____
_____
_____
_____
_____

NIGHTLY GRATITUDE:_____
_____
_____
_____
_____
_____

September 12

DAILY FOCUS: _____

DAILY COMMITMENT: _____
_____
_____

DAILY TOP TARGET: _____
_____
_____
_____

DAILY FOCUSED MEDITATION:

"I breathe in _____, I breathe out _____."

DAILY GOALS: **DAILY FOCUS:**

_____   _____
_____   _____
_____   _____
_____   _____
_____   _____
_____   _____
_____   _____
_____   _____
_____   _____
_____   _____

NIGHTLY SUCCESS RECAP: _____
_____
_____
_____
_____
_____

NIGHTLY GRATITUDE:_____
_____
_____
_____
_____
_____
_____

September 13

DAILY FOCUS: _____

DAILY COMMITMENT: _____
_____
_____

DAILY TOP TARGET: _____
_____
_____
_____

DAILY FOCUSED MEDITATION:

"I breathe in _____, I breathe out _____."

DAILY GOALS:

_____
_____
_____
_____
_____
_____
_____
_____
_____

DAILY FOCUS:

_____
_____
_____
_____
_____
_____
_____
_____
_____

NIGHTLY SUCCESS RECAP: _____
_____
_____
_____
_____
_____

NIGHTLY GRATITUDE: _____
_____
_____
_____
_____
_____
_____

September 14

DAILY FOCUS: _____

DAILY COMMITMENT: _____
_____
_____

DAILY TOP TARGET: _____
_____
_____
_____

DAILY FOCUSED MEDITATION:

"I breathe in _____, I breathe out _____."

DAILY GOALS:	DAILY FOCUS:
_____	_____
_____	_____
_____	_____
_____	_____
_____	_____
_____	_____
_____	_____
_____	_____
_____	_____
_____	_____

NIGHTLY SUCCESS RECAP: _____
_____
_____
_____
_____
_____

NIGHTLY GRATITUDE: _____
_____
_____
_____
_____
_____
_____

September 15

DAILY FOCUS: _____

DAILY COMMITMENT: _____
_____
_____

DAILY TOP TARGET: _____
_____
_____
_____

DAILY FOCUSED MEDITATION:

"I breathe in _____, I breathe out _____."

DAILY GOALS:	DAILY FOCUS:
_____	_____
_____	_____
_____	_____
_____	_____
_____	_____
_____	_____
_____	_____
_____	_____
_____	_____

NIGHTLY SUCCESS RECAP: _____
_____
_____
_____
_____
_____

NIGHTLY GRATITUDE: _____
_____
_____
_____
_____
_____
_____

September 16

DAILY FOCUS: _____

DAILY COMMITMENT: _____
_____
_____

DAILY TOP TARGET: _____
_____
_____
_____

DAILY FOCUSED MEDITATION:

"I breathe in _____, I breathe out _____."

DAILY GOALS: **DAILY FOCUS:**

_____   _____
_____   _____
_____   _____
_____   _____
_____   _____
_____   _____
_____   _____
_____   _____
_____   _____

NIGHTLY SUCCESS RECAP: _____
_____
_____
_____
_____
_____

NIGHTLY GRATITUDE: _____
_____
_____
_____
_____
_____
_____

September 17

DAILY FOCUS: _____

DAILY COMMITMENT: _____
_____
_____

DAILY TOP TARGET: _____
_____
_____
_____

DAILY FOCUSED MEDITATION:

"I breathe in _____, I breathe out _____."

DAILY GOALS:	**DAILY FOCUS:**
_____	_____
_____	_____
_____	_____
_____	_____
_____	_____
_____	_____
_____	_____
_____	_____
_____	_____

NIGHTLY SUCCESS RECAP: _____
_____
_____
_____
_____
_____

NIGHTLY GRATITUDE: _____
_____
_____
_____
_____
_____
_____

September 18

DAILY FOCUS: _____

DAILY COMMITMENT: _____
_____
_____

DAILY TOP TARGET: _____
_____
_____
_____

DAILY FOCUSED MEDITATION:

"I breathe in _____, I breathe out _____."

DAILY GOALS:	**DAILY FOCUS:**
_____	_____
_____	_____
_____	_____
_____	_____
_____	_____
_____	_____
_____	_____
_____	_____
_____	_____

NIGHTLY SUCCESS RECAP: _____
_____
_____
_____
_____
_____

NIGHTLY GRATITUDE: _____
_____
_____
_____
_____
_____

September 19

DAILY FOCUS: _____

DAILY COMMITMENT: _____
_____
_____

DAILY TOP TARGET: _____
_____
_____
_____

DAILY FOCUSED MEDITATION:

"I breathe in _____, I breathe out _____."

DAILY GOALS:

_____
_____
_____
_____
_____
_____
_____
_____
_____

DAILY FOCUS:

_____
_____
_____
_____
_____
_____
_____
_____
_____

NIGHTLY SUCCESS RECAP: _____
_____
_____
_____
_____
_____

NIGHTLY GRATITUDE: _____
_____
_____
_____
_____
_____
_____

September 20

DAILY FOCUS: _____

DAILY COMMITMENT: _____
_____
_____

DAILY TOP TARGET: _____
_____
_____
_____

DAILY FOCUSED MEDITATION:

"I breathe in _____, I breathe out _____."

DAILY GOALS: **DAILY FOCUS:**

_____   _____
_____   _____
_____   _____
_____   _____
_____   _____
_____   _____
_____   _____
_____   _____
_____   _____

NIGHTLY SUCCESS RECAP: _____
_____
_____
_____
_____
_____

NIGHTLY GRATITUDE: _____
_____
_____
_____
_____
_____

September 21

DAILY FOCUS: _____

DAILY COMMITMENT: _____
_____
_____

DAILY TOP TARGET: _____
_____
_____
_____

DAILY FOCUSED MEDITATION:

"I breathe in _____, I breathe out _____."

DAILY GOALS: **DAILY FOCUS:**

_____   _____
_____   _____
_____   _____
_____   _____
_____   _____
_____   _____
_____   _____
_____   _____
_____   _____

NIGHTLY SUCCESS RECAP: _____
_____
_____
_____
_____
_____

NIGHTLY GRATITUDE:_____
_____
_____
_____
_____
_____
_____

DAILY FOCUS: _____

DAILY COMMITMENT: _____
_____
_____

DAILY TOP TARGET: _____
_____
_____
_____

DAILY FOCUSED MEDITATION:

"I breathe in _____, I breathe out _____."

DAILY GOALS: **DAILY FOCUS:**

_____   _____
_____   _____
_____   _____
_____   _____
_____   _____
_____   _____
_____   _____
_____   _____
_____   _____
_____   _____

NIGHTLY SUCCESS RECAP: _____
_____
_____
_____
_____
_____

NIGHTLY GRATITUDE: _____
_____
_____
_____
_____
_____
_____

September 23

DAILY FOCUS: _____

DAILY COMMITMENT: _____
_____
_____

DAILY TOP TARGET: _____
_____
_____
_____

DAILY FOCUSED MEDITATION:

"I breathe in _____, I breathe out _____."

DAILY GOALS:	**DAILY FOCUS:**
_____	_____
_____	_____
_____	_____
_____	_____
_____	_____
_____	_____
_____	_____
_____	_____
_____	_____

NIGHTLY SUCCESS RECAP: _____
_____
_____
_____
_____
_____

NIGHTLY GRATITUDE: _____
_____
_____
_____
_____
_____

September 24

DAILY FOCUS: _____

DAILY COMMITMENT: _____
_____
_____

DAILY TOP TARGET: _____
_____
_____
_____

DAILY FOCUSED MEDITATION:

"I breathe in _____, I breathe out _____."

DAILY GOALS:	**DAILY FOCUS:**
_____	_____
_____	_____
_____	_____
_____	_____
_____	_____
_____	_____
_____	_____
_____	_____
_____	_____

NIGHTLY SUCCESS RECAP: _____
_____
_____
_____
_____
_____

NIGHTLY GRATITUDE: _____
_____
_____
_____
_____
_____

September 25

DAILY FOCUS: _____

DAILY COMMITMENT: _____
_____
_____

DAILY TOP TARGET: _____
_____
_____
_____

DAILY FOCUSED MEDITATION:

"I breathe in _____, I breathe out _____."

DAILY GOALS:	DAILY FOCUS:
_____	_____
_____	_____
_____	_____
_____	_____
_____	_____
_____	_____
_____	_____
_____	_____
_____	_____

NIGHTLY SUCCESS RECAP: _____
_____
_____
_____
_____
_____

NIGHTLY GRATITUDE: _____
_____
_____
_____
_____
_____
_____

September 26

DAILY FOCUS: _____

DAILY COMMITMENT: _____
_____
_____

DAILY TOP TARGET: _____
_____
_____
_____

DAILY FOCUSED MEDITATION:

"I breathe in _____, I breathe out _____."

DAILY GOALS: **DAILY FOCUS:**

_____   _____
_____   _____
_____   _____
_____   _____
_____   _____
_____   _____
_____   _____
_____   _____
_____   _____

NIGHTLY SUCCESS RECAP: _____
_____
_____
_____
_____
_____

NIGHTLY GRATITUDE: _____
_____
_____
_____
_____
_____

September 27

DAILY FOCUS: _____

DAILY COMMITMENT: _____
_____
_____

DAILY TOP TARGET: _____
_____
_____
_____

DAILY FOCUSED MEDITATION:

"I breathe in _____, I breathe out _____."

DAILY GOALS:	**DAILY FOCUS:**
_____	_____
_____	_____
_____	_____
_____	_____
_____	_____
_____	_____
_____	_____
_____	_____
_____	_____

NIGHTLY SUCCESS RECAP: _____
_____
_____
_____
_____
_____

NIGHTLY GRATITUDE: _____
_____
_____
_____
_____
_____
_____

September 28

DAILY FOCUS: _____

DAILY COMMITMENT: _____
_____
_____

DAILY TOP TARGET: _____
_____
_____
_____

DAILY FOCUSED MEDITATION:

"I breathe in _____, I breathe out _____."

<table>
<tr><td align="center">DAILY GOALS:</td><td align="center">DAILY FOCUS:</td></tr>
</table>

DAILY GOALS:
_____
_____
_____
_____
_____
_____
_____
_____
_____

DAILY FOCUS:
_____
_____
_____
_____
_____
_____
_____
_____
_____

NIGHTLY SUCCESS RECAP: _____
_____
_____
_____
_____
_____
_____

NIGHTLY GRATITUDE: _____
_____
_____
_____
_____
_____
_____

September 29

DAILY FOCUS: _____

DAILY COMMITMENT: _____
_____
_____

DAILY TOP TARGET: _____
_____
_____
_____

DAILY FOCUSED MEDITATION:

"I breathe in _____, I breathe out _____."

DAILY GOALS:	DAILY FOCUS:
_____	_____
_____	_____
_____	_____
_____	_____
_____	_____
_____	_____
_____	_____
_____	_____
_____	_____

NIGHTLY SUCCESS RECAP: _____
_____
_____
_____
_____
_____

NIGHTLY GRATITUDE: _____
_____
_____
_____
_____
_____

September 30

DAILY FOCUS: _____

DAILY COMMITMENT: _____
_____
_____

DAILY TOP TARGET: _____
_____
_____
_____

DAILY FOCUSED MEDITATION:

"I breathe in _____, I breathe out _____."

DAILY GOALS: **DAILY FOCUS:**

_____   _____
_____   _____
_____   _____
_____   _____
_____   _____
_____   _____
_____   _____
_____   _____
_____   _____

NIGHTLY SUCCESS RECAP: _____
_____
_____
_____
_____
_____

NIGHTLY GRATITUDE: _____
_____
_____
_____
_____
_____
_____

October 1

DAILY FOCUS: _____

DAILY COMMITMENT: _____
_____
_____

DAILY TOP TARGET: _____
_____
_____
_____

DAILY FOCUSED MEDITATION:

"I breathe in _____, I breathe out _____."

DAILY GOALS:	DAILY FOCUS:
_____	_____
_____	_____
_____	_____
_____	_____
_____	_____
_____	_____
_____	_____
_____	_____
_____	_____

NIGHTLY SUCCESS RECAP: _____
_____
_____
_____
_____
_____

NIGHTLY GRATITUDE:_____
_____
_____
_____
_____
_____
_____

October 2

DAILY FOCUS: _____

DAILY COMMITMENT: _____
_____
_____

DAILY TOP TARGET: _____
_____
_____
_____

DAILY FOCUSED MEDITATION:

"I breathe in _____, I breathe out _____."

DAILY GOALS:	**DAILY FOCUS:**
_____	_____
_____	_____
_____	_____
_____	_____
_____	_____
_____	_____
_____	_____
_____	_____
_____	_____

NIGHTLY SUCCESS RECAP: _____
_____
_____
_____
_____
_____

NIGHTLY GRATITUDE:_____
_____
_____
_____
_____
_____

October 3

DAILY FOCUS: _____

DAILY COMMITMENT: _____
_____
_____

DAILY TOP TARGET: _____
_____
_____
_____

DAILY FOCUSED MEDITATION:

"I breathe in _____, I breathe out _____."

DAILY GOALS:	DAILY FOCUS:
_____	_____
_____	_____
_____	_____
_____	_____
_____	_____
_____	_____
_____	_____
_____	_____
_____	_____

NIGHTLY SUCCESS RECAP: _____
_____
_____
_____
_____
_____

NIGHTLY GRATITUDE: _____
_____
_____
_____
_____
_____
_____

October 4

DAILY FOCUS: _____

DAILY COMMITMENT: _____
_____
_____

DAILY TOP TARGET: _____
_____
_____
_____

DAILY FOCUSED MEDITATION:

"I breathe in _____, I breathe out _____."

DAILY GOALS:	**DAILY FOCUS:**
_____	_____
_____	_____
_____	_____
_____	_____
_____	_____
_____	_____
_____	_____
_____	_____
_____	_____

NIGHTLY SUCCESS RECAP: _____
_____
_____
_____
_____
_____

NIGHTLY GRATITUDE: _____
_____
_____
_____
_____
_____

October 5

DAILY FOCUS: _____

DAILY COMMITMENT: _____
_____
_____

DAILY TOP TARGET: _____
_____
_____
_____

DAILY FOCUSED MEDITATION:

"I breathe in _____, I breathe out _____."

DAILY GOALS:

_____
_____
_____
_____
_____
_____
_____
_____
_____

DAILY FOCUS:

_____
_____
_____
_____
_____
_____
_____
_____
_____

NIGHTLY SUCCESS RECAP: _____
_____
_____
_____
_____
_____

NIGHTLY GRATITUDE:_____
_____
_____
_____
_____
_____
_____

DAILY FOCUS: _____

DAILY COMMITMENT: _____
_____
_____

DAILY TOP TARGET: _____
_____
_____
_____

DAILY FOCUSED MEDITATION:

"I breathe in _____, I breathe out _____."

DAILY GOALS:	**DAILY FOCUS:**
_____	_____
_____	_____
_____	_____
_____	_____
_____	_____
_____	_____
_____	_____
_____	_____
_____	_____
_____	_____

NIGHTLY SUCCESS RECAP: _____
_____
_____
_____
_____
_____

NIGHTLY GRATITUDE: _____
_____
_____
_____
_____
_____

October 7

DAILY FOCUS: _____

DAILY COMMITMENT: _____
_____
_____

DAILY TOP TARGET: _____
_____
_____
_____

DAILY FOCUSED MEDITATION:

"I breathe in _____, I breathe out _____."

DAILY GOALS:	DAILY FOCUS:
_____	_____
_____	_____
_____	_____
_____	_____
_____	_____
_____	_____
_____	_____
_____	_____
_____	_____

NIGHTLY SUCCESS RECAP: _____
_____
_____
_____
_____
_____

NIGHTLY GRATITUDE: _____
_____
_____
_____
_____
_____

October 8

DAILY FOCUS: _____

DAILY COMMITMENT: _____
_____
_____

DAILY TOP TARGET: _____
_____
_____
_____

DAILY FOCUSED MEDITATION:

"I breathe in _____, I breathe out _____."

DAILY GOALS:	**DAILY FOCUS:**
_____	_____
_____	_____
_____	_____
_____	_____
_____	_____
_____	_____
_____	_____
_____	_____
_____	_____
_____	_____

NIGHTLY SUCCESS RECAP: _____
_____
_____
_____
_____
_____

NIGHTLY GRATITUDE: _____
_____
_____
_____
_____
_____

October 9

DAILY FOCUS: _____

DAILY COMMITMENT: _____
_____
_____

DAILY TOP TARGET: _____
_____
_____
_____

DAILY FOCUSED MEDITATION:

"I breathe in _____, I breathe out _____."

<table>
<tr><td align="center">DAILY GOALS:</td><td align="center">DAILY FOCUS:</td></tr>
</table>

DAILY GOALS:	DAILY FOCUS:
_____	_____
_____	_____
_____	_____
_____	_____
_____	_____
_____	_____
_____	_____
_____	_____
_____	_____

NIGHTLY SUCCESS RECAP: _____
_____
_____
_____
_____
_____

NIGHTLY GRATITUDE: _____
_____
_____
_____
_____
_____
_____

October 10

DAILY FOCUS: _____

DAILY COMMITMENT: _____
_____
_____

DAILY TOP TARGET: _____
_____
_____
_____

DAILY FOCUSED MEDITATION:

"I breathe in _____, I breathe out _____."

DAILY GOALS:	**DAILY FOCUS:**
_____	_____
_____	_____
_____	_____
_____	_____
_____	_____
_____	_____
_____	_____
_____	_____
_____	_____

NIGHTLY SUCCESS RECAP: _____
_____
_____
_____
_____
_____

NIGHTLY GRATITUDE: _____
_____
_____
_____
_____
_____

October 11

DAILY FOCUS: _____

DAILY COMMITMENT: _____
_____
_____

DAILY TOP TARGET: _____
_____
_____
_____

DAILY FOCUSED MEDITATION:

"I breathe in _____, I breathe out _____."

DAILY GOALS:	DAILY FOCUS:
_____	_____
_____	_____
_____	_____
_____	_____
_____	_____
_____	_____
_____	_____
_____	_____
_____	_____

NIGHTLY SUCCESS RECAP: _____
_____
_____
_____
_____
_____

NIGHTLY GRATITUDE: _____
_____
_____
_____
_____
_____
_____

October 12

DAILY FOCUS: _____

DAILY COMMITMENT: _____
_____
_____

DAILY TOP TARGET: _____
_____
_____
_____

DAILY FOCUSED MEDITATION:

"I breathe in _____, I breathe out _____."

DAILY GOALS:

_____
_____
_____
_____
_____
_____
_____
_____
_____
_____

DAILY FOCUS:

_____
_____
_____
_____
_____
_____
_____
_____
_____
_____

NIGHTLY SUCCESS RECAP: _____
_____
_____
_____
_____
_____
_____

NIGHTLY GRATITUDE: _____
_____
_____
_____
_____
_____
_____

October 13

DAILY FOCUS: _____

DAILY COMMITMENT: _____
_____
_____

DAILY TOP TARGET: _____
_____
_____
_____

DAILY FOCUSED MEDITATION:

"I breathe in _____, I breathe out _____."

DAILY GOALS:	DAILY FOCUS:
_____	_____
_____	_____
_____	_____
_____	_____
_____	_____
_____	_____
_____	_____
_____	_____
_____	_____

NIGHTLY SUCCESS RECAP: _____
_____
_____
_____
_____
_____

NIGHTLY GRATITUDE: _____
_____
_____
_____
_____
_____
_____

October 14

DAILY FOCUS: _____

DAILY COMMITMENT: _____
_____
_____

DAILY TOP TARGET: _____
_____
_____
_____

DAILY FOCUSED MEDITATION:

"I breathe in _____, I breathe out _____."

DAILY GOALS:	DAILY FOCUS:
_____	_____
_____	_____
_____	_____
_____	_____
_____	_____
_____	_____
_____	_____
_____	_____
_____	_____

NIGHTLY SUCCESS RECAP: _____
_____
_____
_____
_____
_____

NIGHTLY GRATITUDE: _____
_____
_____
_____
_____
_____

October 15

DAILY FOCUS: _____

DAILY COMMITMENT: _____
_____
_____

DAILY TOP TARGET: _____
_____
_____
_____

DAILY FOCUSED MEDITATION:

"I breathe in _____, I breathe out _____."

DAILY GOALS:	**DAILY FOCUS:**
_____	_____
_____	_____
_____	_____
_____	_____
_____	_____
_____	_____
_____	_____
_____	_____
_____	_____

NIGHTLY SUCCESS RECAP: _____
_____
_____
_____
_____
_____
_____

NIGHTLY GRATITUDE:_____
_____
_____
_____
_____
_____
_____

October 16

DAILY FOCUS: _____

DAILY COMMITMENT: _____
_____

DAILY TOP TARGET: _____
_____
_____
_____

DAILY FOCUSED MEDITATION:

"I breathe in _____, I breathe out _____."

DAILY GOALS:

_____
_____
_____
_____
_____
_____
_____
_____
_____

DAILY FOCUS:

_____
_____
_____
_____
_____
_____
_____
_____
_____

NIGHTLY SUCCESS RECAP: _____
_____
_____
_____
_____
_____

NIGHTLY GRATITUDE: _____
_____
_____
_____
_____
_____

October 17

DAILY FOCUS: _____

DAILY COMMITMENT: _____
_____
_____

DAILY TOP TARGET: _____
_____
_____
_____

DAILY FOCUSED MEDITATION:

"I breathe in _____, I breathe out _____."

DAILY GOALS:	**DAILY FOCUS:**
_____	_____
_____	_____
_____	_____
_____	_____
_____	_____
_____	_____
_____	_____
_____	_____
_____	_____
_____	_____

NIGHTLY SUCCESS RECAP: _____
_____
_____
_____
_____
_____

NIGHTLY GRATITUDE: _____
_____
_____
_____
_____
_____
_____

DAILY FOCUS: _____

DAILY COMMITMENT: _____
_____
_____

DAILY TOP TARGET: _____
_____
_____
_____

DAILY FOCUSED MEDITATION:

"I breathe in _____, I breathe out _____."

DAILY GOALS: **DAILY FOCUS:**

_____   _____
_____   _____
_____   _____
_____   _____
_____   _____
_____   _____
_____   _____
_____   _____
_____   _____
_____   _____

NIGHTLY SUCCESS RECAP: _____
_____
_____
_____
_____
_____
_____

NIGHTLY GRATITUDE: _____
_____
_____
_____
_____
_____
_____

October 19

DAILY FOCUS: _____

DAILY COMMITMENT: _____
_____
_____

DAILY TOP TARGET: _____
_____
_____
_____

DAILY FOCUSED MEDITATION:

"I breathe in _____, I breathe out _____."

DAILY GOALS: **DAILY FOCUS:**

_____   _____
_____   _____
_____   _____
_____   _____
_____   _____
_____   _____
_____   _____
_____   _____
_____   _____
_____   _____

NIGHTLY SUCCESS RECAP: _____
_____
_____
_____
_____
_____

NIGHTLY GRATITUDE:_____
_____
_____
_____
_____
_____
_____

October 20

DAILY FOCUS: _____

DAILY COMMITMENT: _____
_____
_____

DAILY TOP TARGET: _____
_____
_____
_____

DAILY FOCUSED MEDITATION:

"I breathe in _____, I breathe out _____."

DAILY GOALS:	**DAILY FOCUS:**
_____	_____
_____	_____
_____	_____
_____	_____
_____	_____
_____	_____
_____	_____
_____	_____
_____	_____

NIGHTLY SUCCESS RECAP: _____
_____
_____
_____
_____
_____

NIGHTLY GRATITUDE: _____
_____
_____
_____
_____
_____

October 21

DAILY FOCUS: _____

DAILY COMMITMENT: _____
_____
_____

DAILY TOP TARGET: _____
_____
_____
_____

DAILY FOCUSED MEDITATION:

"I breathe in _____, I breathe out _____."

<table>
<tr><td>DAILY GOALS:</td><td>DAILY FOCUS:</td></tr>
</table>

DAILY GOALS: DAILY FOCUS:

_____   _____
_____   _____
_____   _____
_____   _____
_____   _____
_____   _____
_____   _____
_____   _____
_____   _____

NIGHTLY SUCCESS RECAP: _____
_____
_____
_____
_____
_____

NIGHTLY GRATITUDE: _____
_____
_____
_____
_____
_____

October 22

DAILY FOCUS: _____

DAILY COMMITMENT: _____
_____
_____

DAILY TOP TARGET: _____
_____
_____
_____

DAILY FOCUSED MEDITATION:

"I breathe in _____, I breathe out _____."

<table>
<tr><td align="center">**DAILY GOALS:**</td><td align="center">**DAILY FOCUS:**</td></tr>
<tr><td>_____</td><td>_____</td></tr>
<tr><td>_____</td><td>_____</td></tr>
<tr><td>_____</td><td>_____</td></tr>
<tr><td>_____</td><td>_____</td></tr>
<tr><td>_____</td><td>_____</td></tr>
<tr><td>_____</td><td>_____</td></tr>
<tr><td>_____</td><td>_____</td></tr>
<tr><td>_____</td><td>_____</td></tr>
<tr><td>_____</td><td>_____</td></tr>
</table>

NIGHTLY SUCCESS RECAP: _____
_____
_____
_____
_____
_____

NIGHTLY GRATITUDE:_____
_____
_____
_____
_____
_____

October 23

DAILY FOCUS: _____

DAILY COMMITMENT: _____
_____
_____

DAILY TOP TARGET: _____
_____
_____
_____

DAILY FOCUSED MEDITATION:

"I breathe in _____, I breathe out _____."

DAILY GOALS:	DAILY FOCUS:
_____	_____
_____	_____
_____	_____
_____	_____
_____	_____
_____	_____
_____	_____
_____	_____
_____	_____

NIGHTLY SUCCESS RECAP: _____
_____
_____
_____
_____
_____

NIGHTLY GRATITUDE:_____
_____
_____
_____
_____
_____
_____

DAILY FOCUS: _____

DAILY COMMITMENT: _____
_____
_____

DAILY TOP TARGET: _____
_____
_____
_____

DAILY FOCUSED MEDITATION:

"I breathe in _____, I breathe out _____."

DAILY GOALS:	**DAILY FOCUS:**
_____	_____
_____	_____
_____	_____
_____	_____
_____	_____
_____	_____
_____	_____
_____	_____
_____	_____

NIGHTLY SUCCESS RECAP: _____
_____
_____
_____
_____
_____

NIGHTLY GRATITUDE: _____
_____
_____
_____
_____
_____

October 25

DAILY FOCUS: _____

DAILY COMMITMENT: _____
_____
_____

DAILY TOP TARGET: _____
_____
_____
_____

DAILY FOCUSED MEDITATION:

"I breathe in _____, I breathe out _____."

DAILY GOALS: DAILY FOCUS:

_____   _____
_____   _____
_____   _____
_____   _____
_____   _____
_____   _____
_____   _____
_____   _____
_____   _____
_____   _____

NIGHTLY SUCCESS RECAP: _____
_____
_____
_____
_____
_____

NIGHTLY GRATITUDE:_____
_____
_____
_____
_____
_____
_____

October 26

DAILY FOCUS: _____

DAILY COMMITMENT: _____
_____
_____

DAILY TOP TARGET: _____
_____
_____
_____

DAILY FOCUSED MEDITATION:

"I breathe in _____, I breathe out _____."

DAILY GOALS:

_____
_____
_____
_____
_____
_____
_____
_____
_____

DAILY FOCUS:

_____
_____
_____
_____
_____
_____
_____
_____
_____

NIGHTLY SUCCESS RECAP: _____
_____
_____
_____
_____
_____

NIGHTLY GRATITUDE: _____
_____
_____
_____
_____
_____

October 27

DAILY FOCUS: _____

DAILY COMMITMENT: _____
_____
_____

DAILY TOP TARGET: _____
_____
_____
_____

DAILY FOCUSED MEDITATION:

"I breathe in _____, I breathe out _____."

DAILY GOALS:	DAILY FOCUS:
_____	_____
_____	_____
_____	_____
_____	_____
_____	_____
_____	_____
_____	_____
_____	_____
_____	_____

NIGHTLY SUCCESS RECAP: _____
_____
_____
_____
_____
_____

NIGHTLY GRATITUDE: _____
_____
_____
_____
_____
_____

DAILY FOCUS: _____

DAILY COMMITMENT: _____
_____
_____

DAILY TOP TARGET: _____
_____
_____
_____

DAILY FOCUSED MEDITATION:

"I breathe in _____, I breathe out _____."

DAILY GOALS:	DAILY FOCUS:
_____	_____
_____	_____
_____	_____
_____	_____
_____	_____
_____	_____
_____	_____
_____	_____
_____	_____

NIGHTLY SUCCESS RECAP: _____
_____
_____
_____
_____
_____

NIGHTLY GRATITUDE: _____
_____
_____
_____
_____
_____

October 29

DAILY FOCUS: _____

DAILY COMMITMENT: _____
_____
_____

DAILY TOP TARGET: _____
_____
_____
_____

DAILY FOCUSED MEDITATION:

"I breathe in _____, I breathe out _____."

DAILY GOALS: **DAILY FOCUS:**

_____   _____
_____   _____
_____   _____
_____   _____
_____   _____
_____   _____
_____   _____
_____   _____

NIGHTLY SUCCESS RECAP: _____
_____
_____
_____
_____
_____

NIGHTLY GRATITUDE:_____
_____
_____
_____
_____
_____
_____

October 30

DAILY FOCUS: _____

DAILY COMMITMENT: _____
_____
_____

DAILY TOP TARGET: _____
_____
_____
_____

DAILY FOCUSED MEDITATION:

"I breathe in _____, I breathe out _____."

DAILY GOALS:	DAILY FOCUS:
_____	_____
_____	_____
_____	_____
_____	_____
_____	_____
_____	_____
_____	_____
_____	_____
_____	_____

NIGHTLY SUCCESS RECAP: _____
_____
_____
_____
_____
_____

NIGHTLY GRATITUDE: _____
_____
_____
_____
_____
_____

October 31

DAILY FOCUS: _____

DAILY COMMITMENT: _____
_____
_____

DAILY TOP TARGET: _____
_____
_____
_____

DAILY FOCUSED MEDITATION:

"I breathe in _____, I breathe out _____."

DAILY GOALS:	DAILY FOCUS:
_____	_____
_____	_____
_____	_____
_____	_____
_____	_____
_____	_____
_____	_____
_____	_____
_____	_____
_____	_____

NIGHTLY SUCCESS RECAP: _____
_____
_____
_____
_____
_____

NIGHTLY GRATITUDE: _____
_____
_____
_____
_____
_____
_____

November 1

DAILY FOCUS: _____

DAILY COMMITMENT: _____
_____
_____

DAILY TOP TARGET: _____
_____
_____
_____

DAILY FOCUSED MEDITATION:

"I breathe in _____, I breathe out _____."

DAILY GOALS:	**DAILY FOCUS:**
_____	_____
_____	_____
_____	_____
_____	_____
_____	_____
_____	_____
_____	_____
_____	_____
_____	_____
_____	_____

NIGHTLY SUCCESS RECAP: _____
_____
_____
_____
_____
_____
_____

NIGHTLY GRATITUDE: _____
_____
_____
_____
_____
_____
_____

November 2

DAILY FOCUS: _____

DAILY COMMITMENT: _____
_____
_____

DAILY TOP TARGET: _____
_____
_____
_____

DAILY FOCUSED MEDITATION:

"I breathe in _____, I breathe out _____."

DAILY GOALS:	**DAILY FOCUS:**
_____	_____
_____	_____
_____	_____
_____	_____
_____	_____
_____	_____
_____	_____
_____	_____
_____	_____

NIGHTLY SUCCESS RECAP: _____
_____
_____
_____
_____
_____

NIGHTLY GRATITUDE: _____
_____
_____
_____
_____
_____
_____

November 3

DAILY FOCUS: _____

DAILY COMMITMENT: _____
_____
_____

DAILY TOP TARGET: _____
_____
_____
_____

DAILY FOCUSED MEDITATION:

"I breathe in _____, I breathe out _____."

DAILY GOALS: **DAILY FOCUS:**

_____   _____
_____   _____
_____   _____
_____   _____
_____   _____
_____   _____
_____   _____
_____   _____
_____   _____
_____   _____

NIGHTLY SUCCESS RECAP: _____
_____
_____
_____
_____
_____
_____

NIGHTLY GRATITUDE: _____
_____
_____
_____
_____
_____
_____

November 4

DAILY FOCUS: _____

DAILY COMMITMENT: _____
_____
_____

DAILY TOP TARGET: _____
_____
_____
_____

DAILY FOCUSED MEDITATION:

"I breathe in _____, I breathe out _____."

DAILY GOALS:	**DAILY FOCUS:**
_____	_____
_____	_____
_____	_____
_____	_____
_____	_____
_____	_____
_____	_____
_____	_____
_____	_____
_____	_____

NIGHTLY SUCCESS RECAP: _____
_____
_____
_____
_____
_____

NIGHTLY GRATITUDE: _____
_____
_____
_____
_____
_____

November 5

DAILY FOCUS: _____

DAILY COMMITMENT: _____
_____
_____

DAILY TOP TARGET: _____
_____
_____
_____

DAILY FOCUSED MEDITATION:

"I breathe in _____, I breathe out _____."

DAILY GOALS:	**DAILY FOCUS:**

NIGHTLY SUCCESS RECAP: _____
_____
_____
_____
_____
_____

NIGHTLY GRATITUDE: _____
_____
_____
_____
_____
_____

November 6

DAILY FOCUS: _____

DAILY COMMITMENT: _____
_____
_____

DAILY TOP TARGET: _____
_____
_____
_____

DAILY FOCUSED MEDITATION:

"I breathe in _____, I breathe out _____."

DAILY GOALS:

_____
_____
_____
_____
_____
_____
_____
_____

DAILY FOCUS:

_____
_____
_____
_____
_____
_____
_____
_____

NIGHTLY SUCCESS RECAP: _____
_____
_____
_____
_____
_____

NIGHTLY GRATITUDE: _____
_____
_____
_____
_____
_____
_____

DAILY FOCUS: _____

DAILY COMMITMENT: _____
_____
_____

DAILY TOP TARGET: _____
_____
_____
_____

DAILY FOCUSED MEDITATION:

"I breathe in _____**, I breathe out** _____**."**

DAILY GOALS:	**DAILY FOCUS:**
_____	_____
_____	_____
_____	_____
_____	_____
_____	_____
_____	_____
_____	_____
_____	_____
_____	_____
_____	_____

NIGHTLY SUCCESS RECAP: _____
_____
_____
_____
_____
_____

NIGHTLY GRATITUDE:_____
_____
_____
_____
_____
_____

November 8

DAILY FOCUS: _____

DAILY COMMITMENT: _____
_____
_____

DAILY TOP TARGET: _____
_____
_____
_____

DAILY FOCUSED MEDITATION:

"I breathe in _____, I breathe out _____."

DAILY GOALS:	DAILY FOCUS:
_____	_____
_____	_____
_____	_____
_____	_____
_____	_____
_____	_____
_____	_____
_____	_____

NIGHTLY SUCCESS RECAP: _____
_____
_____
_____
_____
_____

NIGHTLY GRATITUDE:_____
_____
_____
_____
_____
_____
_____

DAILY FOCUS: _____

DAILY COMMITMENT: _____
_____
_____

DAILY TOP TARGET: _____
_____
_____
_____

DAILY FOCUSED MEDITATION:

"I breathe in _____, I breathe out _____."

DAILY GOALS: **DAILY FOCUS:**

_____   _____
_____   _____
_____   _____
_____   _____
_____   _____
_____   _____
_____   _____
_____   _____
_____   _____

NIGHTLY SUCCESS RECAP: _____
_____
_____
_____
_____
_____

NIGHTLY GRATITUDE: _____
_____
_____
_____
_____
_____

November 10

DAILY FOCUS: _____

DAILY COMMITMENT: _____
_____
_____

DAILY TOP TARGET: _____
_____
_____
_____

DAILY FOCUSED MEDITATION:

"I breathe in _____, I breathe out _____."

DAILY GOALS:	**DAILY FOCUS:**
_____	_____
_____	_____
_____	_____
_____	_____
_____	_____
_____	_____
_____	_____
_____	_____
_____	_____

NIGHTLY SUCCESS RECAP: _____
_____
_____
_____
_____
_____
_____

NIGHTLY GRATITUDE: _____
_____
_____
_____
_____
_____
_____

November 11

DAILY FOCUS: _____

DAILY COMMITMENT: _____
_____
_____

DAILY TOP TARGET: _____
_____
_____
_____

DAILY FOCUSED MEDITATION:

"I breathe in _____, I breathe out _____."

DAILY GOALS:	**DAILY FOCUS:**
_____	_____
_____	_____
_____	_____
_____	_____
_____	_____
_____	_____
_____	_____
_____	_____
_____	_____
_____	_____

NIGHTLY SUCCESS RECAP: _____
_____
_____
_____
_____
_____

NIGHTLY GRATITUDE: _____
_____
_____
_____
_____
_____

November 12

DAILY FOCUS: _____

DAILY COMMITMENT: _____
_____
_____

DAILY TOP TARGET: _____
_____
_____
_____

DAILY FOCUSED MEDITATION:

"I breathe in _____, I breathe out _____."

DAILY GOALS:

_____
_____
_____
_____
_____
_____
_____
_____
_____

DAILY FOCUS:

_____
_____
_____
_____
_____
_____
_____
_____
_____

NIGHTLY SUCCESS RECAP: _____
_____
_____
_____
_____
_____

NIGHTLY GRATITUDE:_____
_____
_____
_____
_____
_____
_____

November 13

DAILY FOCUS: _____

DAILY COMMITMENT: _____
_____
_____

DAILY TOP TARGET: _____
_____
_____
_____

DAILY FOCUSED MEDITATION:

"I breathe in _____, I breathe out _____."

DAILY GOALS:	DAILY FOCUS:
_____	_____
_____	_____
_____	_____
_____	_____
_____	_____
_____	_____
_____	_____
_____	_____
_____	_____

NIGHTLY SUCCESS RECAP: _____
_____
_____
_____
_____
_____
_____

NIGHTLY GRATITUDE: _____
_____
_____
_____
_____
_____
_____

November 14

DAILY FOCUS: _____

DAILY COMMITMENT: _____
_____
_____

DAILY TOP TARGET: _____
_____
_____
_____

DAILY FOCUSED MEDITATION:

"I breathe in _____, I breathe out _____."

DAILY GOALS: **DAILY FOCUS:**

NIGHTLY SUCCESS RECAP: _____
_____
_____
_____
_____
_____

NIGHTLY GRATITUDE: _____
_____
_____
_____
_____
_____
_____

November 15

DAILY FOCUS: _____

DAILY COMMITMENT: _____
_____
_____

DAILY TOP TARGET: _____
_____
_____
_____

DAILY FOCUSED MEDITATION:

"I breathe in _____, I breathe out _____."

DAILY GOALS:

_____
_____
_____
_____
_____
_____
_____
_____
_____

DAILY FOCUS:

_____
_____
_____
_____
_____
_____
_____
_____
_____

NIGHTLY SUCCESS RECAP: _____
_____
_____
_____
_____
_____

NIGHTLY GRATITUDE: _____
_____
_____
_____
_____
_____

November 16

DAILY FOCUS: _____

DAILY COMMITMENT: _____
_____
_____

DAILY TOP TARGET: _____
_____
_____
_____

DAILY FOCUSED MEDITATION:

"I breathe in _____, I breathe out _____."

DAILY GOALS:

_____
_____
_____
_____
_____
_____
_____
_____
_____
_____

DAILY FOCUS:

_____
_____
_____
_____
_____
_____
_____
_____
_____
_____

NIGHTLY SUCCESS RECAP: _____
_____
_____
_____
_____
_____
_____

NIGHTLY GRATITUDE: _____
_____
_____
_____
_____
_____
_____

November 17

DAILY FOCUS: _____

DAILY COMMITMENT: _____
_____
_____

DAILY TOP TARGET: _____
_____
_____
_____

DAILY FOCUSED MEDITATION:

"I breathe in _____, I breathe out _____."

          DAILY GOALS: **DAILY FOCUS:**

_____   _____
_____   _____
_____   _____
_____   _____
_____   _____
_____   _____
_____   _____
_____   _____
_____   _____

NIGHTLY SUCCESS RECAP: _____
_____
_____
_____
_____
_____
_____

NIGHTLY GRATITUDE: _____
_____
_____
_____
_____
_____
_____

November 18

DAILY FOCUS: _____

DAILY COMMITMENT: _____
_____
_____

DAILY TOP TARGET: _____
_____
_____
_____

DAILY FOCUSED MEDITATION:

"I breathe in _____, I breathe out _____."

DAILY GOALS:

_____
_____
_____
_____
_____
_____
_____
_____
_____

DAILY FOCUS:

_____
_____
_____
_____
_____
_____
_____
_____
_____

NIGHTLY SUCCESS RECAP: _____
_____
_____
_____
_____
_____

NIGHTLY GRATITUDE: _____
_____
_____
_____
_____
_____

November 19

DAILY FOCUS: _____

DAILY COMMITMENT: _____
_____
_____

DAILY TOP TARGET: _____
_____
_____
_____

DAILY FOCUSED MEDITATION:

"I breathe in _____, I breathe out _____."

DAILY GOALS:	DAILY FOCUS:
_____	_____
_____	_____
_____	_____
_____	_____
_____	_____
_____	_____
_____	_____
_____	_____
_____	_____

NIGHTLY SUCCESS RECAP: _____
_____
_____
_____
_____
_____
_____

NIGHTLY GRATITUDE: _____
_____
_____
_____
_____
_____
_____

November 20

DAILY FOCUS: _____

DAILY COMMITMENT: _____
_____
_____

DAILY TOP TARGET: _____
_____
_____
_____

DAILY FOCUSED MEDITATION:

"I breathe in _____, I breathe out _____."

DAILY GOALS:	**DAILY FOCUS:**
_____	_____
_____	_____
_____	_____
_____	_____
_____	_____
_____	_____
_____	_____
_____	_____
_____	_____

NIGHTLY SUCCESS RECAP: _____
_____
_____
_____
_____
_____

NIGHTLY GRATITUDE: _____
_____
_____
_____
_____
_____

November 21

DAILY FOCUS: _____

DAILY COMMITMENT: _____
_____
_____

DAILY TOP TARGET: _____
_____
_____
_____

DAILY FOCUSED MEDITATION:

"I breathe in _____, I breathe out _____."

DAILY GOALS:	DAILY FOCUS:
_____	_____
_____	_____
_____	_____
_____	_____
_____	_____
_____	_____
_____	_____
_____	_____
_____	_____

NIGHTLY SUCCESS RECAP: _____
_____
_____
_____
_____
_____

NIGHTLY GRATITUDE: _____
_____
_____
_____
_____
_____

November 22

DAILY FOCUS: _____

DAILY COMMITMENT: _____
_____
_____

DAILY TOP TARGET: _____
_____
_____
_____

DAILY FOCUSED MEDITATION:

"I breathe in _____, I breathe out _____."

DAILY GOALS:

_____
_____
_____
_____
_____
_____
_____
_____
_____

DAILY FOCUS:

_____
_____
_____
_____
_____
_____
_____
_____
_____

NIGHTLY SUCCESS RECAP: _____
_____
_____
_____
_____
_____
_____

NIGHTLY GRATITUDE: _____
_____
_____
_____
_____
_____
_____

November 23

DAILY FOCUS: _____

DAILY COMMITMENT: _____
_____
_____

DAILY TOP TARGET: _____
_____
_____
_____

DAILY FOCUSED MEDITATION:

"I breathe in _____, I breathe out _____."

DAILY GOALS: **DAILY FOCUS:**

_____   _____
_____   _____
_____   _____
_____   _____
_____   _____
_____   _____
_____   _____
_____   _____
_____   _____

NIGHTLY SUCCESS RECAP: _____
_____
_____
_____
_____
_____

NIGHTLY GRATITUDE: _____
_____
_____
_____
_____
_____

November 24

DAILY FOCUS: _____

DAILY COMMITMENT: _____
_____
_____

DAILY TOP TARGET: _____
_____
_____
_____

DAILY FOCUSED MEDITATION:

"I breathe in _____, I breathe out _____."

DAILY GOALS:	**DAILY FOCUS:**
_____	_____
_____	_____
_____	_____
_____	_____
_____	_____
_____	_____
_____	_____
_____	_____
_____	_____

NIGHTLY SUCCESS RECAP: _____
_____
_____
_____
_____
_____

NIGHTLY GRATITUDE:_____
_____
_____
_____
_____
_____

DAILY FOCUS: _____

DAILY COMMITMENT: _____
_____
_____

DAILY TOP TARGET: _____
_____
_____
_____

DAILY FOCUSED MEDITATION:

"I breathe in _____, I breathe out _____."

DAILY GOALS:

_____
_____
_____
_____
_____
_____
_____
_____
_____
_____

DAILY FOCUS:

_____
_____
_____
_____
_____
_____
_____
_____
_____
_____

NIGHTLY SUCCESS RECAP: _____
_____
_____
_____
_____
_____

NIGHTLY GRATITUDE: _____
_____
_____
_____
_____
_____

November 26

DAILY FOCUS: _____

DAILY COMMITMENT: _____
_____
_____

DAILY TOP TARGET: _____
_____
_____
_____

DAILY FOCUSED MEDITATION:

"I breathe in _____, I breathe out _____."

DAILY GOALS:	**DAILY FOCUS:**
_____	_____
_____	_____
_____	_____
_____	_____
_____	_____
_____	_____
_____	_____
_____	_____

NIGHTLY SUCCESS RECAP: _____
_____
_____
_____
_____
_____
_____

NIGHTLY GRATITUDE: _____
_____
_____
_____
_____
_____

DAILY FOCUS: _____

DAILY COMMITMENT: _____
_____
_____

DAILY TOP TARGET: _____
_____
_____
_____

DAILY FOCUSED MEDITATION:

"I breathe in _____, I breathe out _____."

DAILY GOALS:

_____
_____
_____
_____
_____
_____
_____
_____
_____

DAILY FOCUS:

_____
_____
_____
_____
_____
_____
_____
_____
_____

NIGHTLY SUCCESS RECAP: _____
_____
_____
_____
_____
_____

NIGHTLY GRATITUDE: _____
_____
_____
_____
_____
_____

November 28

DAILY FOCUS: _____

DAILY COMMITMENT: _____
_____
_____

DAILY TOP TARGET: _____
_____
_____
_____

DAILY FOCUSED MEDITATION:

"I breathe in _____, I breathe out _____."

DAILY GOALS:

_____
_____
_____
_____
_____
_____
_____
_____
_____
_____

DAILY FOCUS:

_____
_____
_____
_____
_____
_____
_____
_____
_____
_____

NIGHTLY SUCCESS RECAP: _____
_____
_____
_____
_____
_____
_____

NIGHTLY GRATITUDE: _____
_____
_____
_____
_____
_____
_____

DAILY FOCUS: _____

DAILY COMMITMENT: _____
_____
_____

DAILY TOP TARGET: _____
_____
_____
_____

DAILY FOCUSED MEDITATION:

"I breathe in _____ **, I breathe out** _____ **."**

DAILY GOALS:	**DAILY FOCUS:**
_____	_____
_____	_____
_____	_____
_____	_____
_____	_____
_____	_____
_____	_____
_____	_____

NIGHTLY SUCCESS RECAP: _____
_____
_____
_____
_____
_____

NIGHTLY GRATITUDE:_____
_____
_____
_____
_____
_____

November 30

DAILY FOCUS: _____

DAILY COMMITMENT: _____
_____
_____

DAILY TOP TARGET: _____
_____
_____
_____

DAILY FOCUSED MEDITATION:

"I breathe in _____, I breathe out _____."

DAILY GOALS:	DAILY FOCUS:
_____	_____
_____	_____
_____	_____
_____	_____
_____	_____
_____	_____
_____	_____
_____	_____
_____	_____

NIGHTLY SUCCESS RECAP: _____
_____
_____
_____
_____
_____
_____

NIGHTLY GRATITUDE: _____
_____
_____
_____
_____
_____
_____

December 1

DAILY FOCUS: _____

DAILY COMMITMENT: _____
_____
_____

DAILY TOP TARGET: _____
_____
_____
_____

DAILY FOCUSED MEDITATION:

"I breathe in _____, I breathe out _____."

<table>
<tr><td align="center">**DAILY GOALS:**</td><td align="center">**DAILY FOCUS:**</td></tr>
</table>

NIGHTLY SUCCESS RECAP: _____
_____
_____
_____
_____
_____

NIGHTLY GRATITUDE: _____
_____
_____
_____
_____
_____

December 2

DAILY FOCUS: _____

DAILY COMMITMENT: _____
_____
_____

DAILY TOP TARGET: _____
_____
_____
_____

DAILY FOCUSED MEDITATION:

"I breathe in _____, I breathe out _____."

DAILY GOALS:	**DAILY FOCUS:**
_____	_____
_____	_____
_____	_____
_____	_____
_____	_____
_____	_____
_____	_____
_____	_____
_____	_____

NIGHTLY SUCCESS RECAP: _____
_____
_____
_____
_____
_____

NIGHTLY GRATITUDE: _____
_____
_____
_____
_____
_____

DAILY FOCUS: _____

DAILY COMMITMENT: _____
_____
_____

DAILY TOP TARGET: _____
_____
_____
_____

DAILY FOCUSED MEDITATION:

"I breathe in _____, I breathe out _____."

DAILY GOALS:	DAILY FOCUS:
_____	_____
_____	_____
_____	_____
_____	_____
_____	_____
_____	_____
_____	_____
_____	_____
_____	_____

NIGHTLY SUCCESS RECAP: _____
_____
_____
_____
_____
_____

NIGHTLY GRATITUDE:_____
_____
_____
_____
_____
_____

December 4

DAILY FOCUS: _____

DAILY COMMITMENT: _____
_____
_____

DAILY TOP TARGET: _____
_____
_____
_____

DAILY FOCUSED MEDITATION:

"I breathe in _____, I breathe out _____."

DAILY GOALS:

_____
_____
_____
_____
_____
_____
_____
_____
_____

DAILY FOCUS:

_____
_____
_____
_____
_____
_____
_____
_____
_____

NIGHTLY SUCCESS RECAP: _____
_____
_____
_____
_____
_____

NIGHTLY GRATITUDE: _____
_____
_____
_____
_____
_____
_____

DAILY FOCUS: _____

DAILY COMMITMENT: _____
_____
_____

DAILY TOP TARGET: _____
_____
_____
_____

DAILY FOCUSED MEDITATION:

"I breathe in _____, I breathe out _____."

DAILY GOALS:	DAILY FOCUS:
_____	_____
_____	_____
_____	_____
_____	_____
_____	_____
_____	_____
_____	_____
_____	_____
_____	_____
_____	_____

NIGHTLY SUCCESS RECAP: _____
_____
_____
_____
_____
_____
_____

NIGHTLY GRATITUDE: _____
_____
_____
_____
_____
_____
_____

December 6

DAILY FOCUS: _____

DAILY COMMITMENT: _____
_____
_____

DAILY TOP TARGET: _____
_____
_____
_____

DAILY FOCUSED MEDITATION:

"I breathe in _____, I breathe out _____."

           DAILY GOALS: **DAILY FOCUS:**

_____   _____
_____   _____
_____   _____
_____   _____
_____   _____
_____   _____
_____   _____
_____   _____
_____   _____

NIGHTLY SUCCESS RECAP: _____
_____
_____
_____
_____
_____

NIGHTLY GRATITUDE: _____
_____
_____
_____
_____
_____

December 7

DAILY FOCUS: _____

DAILY COMMITMENT: _____
_____
_____

DAILY TOP TARGET: _____
_____
_____
_____

DAILY FOCUSED MEDITATION:

"I breathe in _____, I breathe out _____."

DAILY GOALS:	**DAILY FOCUS:**
_____	_____
_____	_____
_____	_____
_____	_____
_____	_____
_____	_____
_____	_____
_____	_____
_____	_____

NIGHTLY SUCCESS RECAP: _____
_____
_____
_____
_____
_____
_____

NIGHTLY GRATITUDE: _____
_____
_____
_____
_____
_____
_____

December 8

DAILY FOCUS: _____

DAILY COMMITMENT: _____
_____
_____

DAILY TOP TARGET: _____
_____
_____
_____

DAILY FOCUSED MEDITATION:

"I breathe in _____, I breathe out _____."

DAILY GOALS:	**DAILY FOCUS:**
_____	_____
_____	_____
_____	_____
_____	_____
_____	_____
_____	_____
_____	_____
_____	_____
_____	_____

NIGHTLY SUCCESS RECAP: _____
_____
_____
_____
_____
_____

NIGHTLY GRATITUDE: _____
_____
_____
_____
_____
_____
_____

DAILY FOCUS: _____

DAILY COMMITMENT: _____
_____
_____

DAILY TOP TARGET: _____
_____
_____
_____

DAILY FOCUSED MEDITATION:

"I breathe in _____, I breathe out _____."

DAILY GOALS:	**DAILY FOCUS:**
_____	_____
_____	_____
_____	_____
_____	_____
_____	_____
_____	_____
_____	_____
_____	_____
_____	_____

NIGHTLY SUCCESS RECAP: _____
_____
_____
_____
_____
_____

NIGHTLY GRATITUDE: _____
_____
_____
_____
_____
_____
_____

December 10

DAILY FOCUS: _____

DAILY COMMITMENT: _____
_____
_____

DAILY TOP TARGET: _____
_____
_____
_____

DAILY FOCUSED MEDITATION:

"I breathe in _____, I breathe out _____."

<table>
<tr><td align="center">DAILY GOALS:</td><td align="center">DAILY FOCUS:</td></tr>
</table>

NIGHTLY SUCCESS RECAP: _____
_____
_____
_____
_____
_____
_____

NIGHTLY GRATITUDE:_____
_____
_____
_____
_____
_____
_____

December 11

DAILY FOCUS: _____

DAILY COMMITMENT: _____
_____
_____

DAILY TOP TARGET: _____
_____
_____
_____

DAILY FOCUSED MEDITATION:

"I breathe in _____ **, I breathe out** _____ **."**

DAILY GOALS:	**DAILY FOCUS:**
_____	_____
_____	_____
_____	_____
_____	_____
_____	_____
_____	_____
_____	_____
_____	_____
_____	_____

NIGHTLY SUCCESS RECAP: _____
_____
_____
_____
_____

NIGHTLY GRATITUDE:_____
_____
_____
_____
_____
_____

December 12

DAILY FOCUS: _____

DAILY COMMITMENT: _____
_____
_____

DAILY TOP TARGET: _____
_____
_____
_____

DAILY FOCUSED MEDITATION:

"I breathe in _____, I breathe out _____."

DAILY GOALS: DAILY FOCUS:

_____   _____
_____   _____
_____   _____
_____   _____
_____   _____
_____   _____
_____   _____
_____   _____
_____   _____

NIGHTLY SUCCESS RECAP: _____
_____
_____
_____
_____
_____
_____

NIGHTLY GRATITUDE: _____
_____
_____
_____
_____
_____
_____

December 13

DAILY FOCUS: _____

DAILY COMMITMENT: _____
_____
_____

DAILY TOP TARGET: _____
_____
_____
_____

DAILY FOCUSED MEDITATION:

"I breathe in _____, I breathe out _____."

DAILY GOALS: **DAILY FOCUS:**

_____   _____
_____   _____
_____   _____
_____   _____
_____   _____
_____   _____
_____   _____
_____   _____
_____   _____

NIGHTLY SUCCESS RECAP: _____
_____
_____
_____
_____
_____

NIGHTLY GRATITUDE: _____
_____
_____
_____
_____
_____
_____

December 14

DAILY FOCUS: _____

DAILY COMMITMENT: _____
_____
_____

DAILY TOP TARGET: _____
_____
_____
_____

DAILY FOCUSED MEDITATION:

"I breathe in _____, I breathe out _____."

DAILY GOALS:	**DAILY FOCUS:**
_____	_____
_____	_____
_____	_____
_____	_____
_____	_____
_____	_____
_____	_____
_____	_____
_____	_____

NIGHTLY SUCCESS RECAP: _____
_____
_____
_____
_____
_____

NIGHTLY GRATITUDE:_____
_____
_____
_____
_____
_____
_____

December 15

DAILY FOCUS: _____

DAILY COMMITMENT: _____
_____
_____

DAILY TOP TARGET: _____
_____
_____
_____

DAILY FOCUSED MEDITATION:

"I breathe in _____, I breathe out _____."

DAILY GOALS:	DAILY FOCUS:
_____	_____
_____	_____
_____	_____
_____	_____
_____	_____
_____	_____
_____	_____
_____	_____
_____	_____
_____	_____

NIGHTLY SUCCESS RECAP: _____
_____
_____
_____
_____
_____

NIGHTLY GRATITUDE: _____
_____
_____
_____
_____
_____

December 16

DAILY FOCUS: _____

DAILY COMMITMENT: _____
_____
_____

DAILY TOP TARGET: _____
_____
_____
_____

DAILY FOCUSED MEDITATION:

"I breathe in _____, I breathe out _____."

DAILY GOALS:	DAILY FOCUS:
_____	_____
_____	_____
_____	_____
_____	_____
_____	_____
_____	_____
_____	_____
_____	_____
_____	_____

NIGHTLY SUCCESS RECAP: _____
_____
_____
_____
_____
_____
_____

NIGHTLY GRATITUDE: _____
_____
_____
_____
_____
_____
_____

December 17

DAILY FOCUS: _____

DAILY COMMITMENT: _____
_____
_____

DAILY TOP TARGET: _____
_____
_____
_____

DAILY FOCUSED MEDITATION:

"I breathe in _____, I breathe out _____."

DAILY GOALS:	**DAILY FOCUS:**
_____	_____
_____	_____
_____	_____
_____	_____
_____	_____
_____	_____
_____	_____
_____	_____
_____	_____

NIGHTLY SUCCESS RECAP: _____
_____
_____
_____
_____
_____

NIGHTLY GRATITUDE: _____
_____
_____
_____
_____
_____
_____

December 18

DAILY FOCUS: _____

DAILY COMMITMENT: _____
_____
_____

DAILY TOP TARGET: _____
_____
_____
_____

DAILY FOCUSED MEDITATION:

"I breathe in _____, I breathe out _____."

DAILY GOALS:	**DAILY FOCUS:**
_____	_____
_____	_____
_____	_____
_____	_____
_____	_____
_____	_____
_____	_____
_____	_____
_____	_____

NIGHTLY SUCCESS RECAP: _____
_____
_____
_____
_____
_____
_____

NIGHTLY GRATITUDE: _____
_____
_____
_____
_____
_____
_____

DAILY FOCUS: _____

DAILY COMMITMENT: _____
_____
_____

DAILY TOP TARGET: _____
_____
_____
_____

DAILY FOCUSED MEDITATION:

"I breathe in _____, I breathe out _____."

DAILY GOALS:	**DAILY FOCUS:**
_____	_____
_____	_____
_____	_____
_____	_____
_____	_____
_____	_____
_____	_____
_____	_____
_____	_____

NIGHTLY SUCCESS RECAP: _____
_____
_____
_____
_____
_____

NIGHTLY GRATITUDE: _____
_____
_____
_____
_____
_____
_____

December 20

DAILY FOCUS: _____

DAILY COMMITMENT: _____
_____
_____

DAILY TOP TARGET: _____
_____
_____
_____

DAILY FOCUSED MEDITATION:

"I breathe in _____, I breathe out _____."

DAILY GOALS:	**DAILY FOCUS:**
_____	_____
_____	_____
_____	_____
_____	_____
_____	_____
_____	_____
_____	_____
_____	_____
_____	_____
_____	_____

NIGHTLY SUCCESS RECAP: _____
_____
_____
_____
_____
_____

NIGHTLY GRATITUDE: _____
_____
_____
_____
_____
_____

December 21

DAILY FOCUS: _____

DAILY COMMITMENT: _____
_____
_____

DAILY TOP TARGET: _____
_____
_____
_____

DAILY FOCUSED MEDITATION:

"I breathe in _____, I breathe out _____."

DAILY GOALS:	**DAILY FOCUS:**
_____	_____
_____	_____
_____	_____
_____	_____
_____	_____
_____	_____
_____	_____
_____	_____
_____	_____
_____	_____

NIGHTLY SUCCESS RECAP: _____
_____
_____
_____
_____

NIGHTLY GRATITUDE: _____
_____
_____
_____
_____
_____

December 22

DAILY FOCUS: _____

DAILY COMMITMENT: _____
_____
_____

DAILY TOP TARGET: _____
_____
_____
_____

DAILY FOCUSED MEDITATION:

"I breathe in _____, I breathe out _____."

DAILY GOALS: DAILY FOCUS:

_____   _____
_____   _____
_____   _____
_____   _____
_____   _____
_____   _____
_____   _____
_____   _____
_____   _____

NIGHTLY SUCCESS RECAP: _____
_____
_____
_____
_____
_____

NIGHTLY GRATITUDE: _____
_____
_____
_____
_____
_____

December 23

DAILY FOCUS: _____

DAILY COMMITMENT: _____
_____
_____

DAILY TOP TARGET: _____
_____
_____
_____

DAILY FOCUSED MEDITATION:

"I breathe in _____, I breathe out _____."

DAILY GOALS: **DAILY FOCUS:**

_____   _____
_____   _____
_____   _____
_____   _____
_____   _____
_____   _____
_____   _____
_____   _____
_____   _____

NIGHTLY SUCCESS RECAP: _____
_____
_____
_____
_____
_____

NIGHTLY GRATITUDE:_____
_____
_____
_____
_____
_____

December 24

DAILY FOCUS: _____

DAILY COMMITMENT: _____
_____
_____

DAILY TOP TARGET: _____
_____
_____
_____

DAILY FOCUSED MEDITATION:

"I breathe in _____, I breathe out _____."

DAILY GOALS:	**DAILY FOCUS:**
_____	_____
_____	_____
_____	_____
_____	_____
_____	_____
_____	_____
_____	_____
_____	_____
_____	_____

NIGHTLY SUCCESS RECAP: _____
_____
_____
_____
_____
_____

NIGHTLY GRATITUDE:_____
_____
_____
_____
_____
_____
_____

December 25

DAILY FOCUS: _____

DAILY COMMITMENT: _____
_____
_____

DAILY TOP TARGET: _____
_____
_____
_____

DAILY FOCUSED MEDITATION:

"I breathe in _____, I breathe out _____."

DAILY GOALS:	DAILY FOCUS:
_____	_____
_____	_____
_____	_____
_____	_____
_____	_____
_____	_____
_____	_____
_____	_____
_____	_____

NIGHTLY SUCCESS RECAP: _____
_____
_____
_____
_____
_____

NIGHTLY GRATITUDE: _____
_____
_____
_____
_____
_____

December 26

DAILY FOCUS: _____

DAILY COMMITMENT: _____
_____
_____

DAILY TOP TARGET: _____
_____
_____
_____

DAILY FOCUSED MEDITATION:

"I breathe in _____, I breathe out _____."

DAILY GOALS:	DAILY FOCUS:
_____	_____
_____	_____
_____	_____
_____	_____
_____	_____
_____	_____
_____	_____
_____	_____
_____	_____

NIGHTLY SUCCESS RECAP: _____
_____
_____
_____
_____
_____
_____

NIGHTLY GRATITUDE:_____
_____
_____
_____
_____
_____
_____

DAILY FOCUS: _____

DAILY COMMITMENT: _____
_____
_____

DAILY TOP TARGET: _____
_____
_____
_____

DAILY FOCUSED MEDITATION:

"I breathe in _____, I breathe out _____."

<table>
<tr><td align="center">**DAILY GOALS:**</td><td align="center">**DAILY FOCUS:**</td></tr>
</table>

DAILY GOALS:	DAILY FOCUS:
_____	_____
_____	_____
_____	_____
_____	_____
_____	_____
_____	_____
_____	_____
_____	_____
_____	_____

NIGHTLY SUCCESS RECAP: _____
_____
_____
_____
_____
_____

NIGHTLY GRATITUDE: _____
_____
_____
_____
_____
_____

December 28

DAILY FOCUS: _____

DAILY COMMITMENT: _____
_____
_____

DAILY TOP TARGET: _____
_____
_____
_____

DAILY FOCUSED MEDITATION:

"I breathe in _____, I breathe out _____."

DAILY GOALS:	DAILY FOCUS:
_____	_____
_____	_____
_____	_____
_____	_____
_____	_____
_____	_____
_____	_____
_____	_____
_____	_____

NIGHTLY SUCCESS RECAP: _____
_____
_____
_____
_____
_____

NIGHTLY GRATITUDE: _____
_____
_____
_____
_____
_____

December 29

DAILY FOCUS: _____

DAILY COMMITMENT: _____
_____
_____

DAILY TOP TARGET: _____
_____
_____
_____

DAILY FOCUSED MEDITATION:

"I breathe in _____, I breathe out _____."

DAILY GOALS:	**DAILY FOCUS:**
_____	_____
_____	_____
_____	_____
_____	_____
_____	_____
_____	_____
_____	_____
_____	_____
_____	_____

NIGHTLY SUCCESS RECAP: _____
_____
_____
_____
_____
_____

NIGHTLY GRATITUDE: _____
_____
_____
_____
_____
_____

December 30

DAILY FOCUS: _____

DAILY COMMITMENT: _____
_____
_____

DAILY TOP TARGET: _____
_____
_____
_____

DAILY FOCUSED MEDITATION:

"I breathe in _____, I breathe out _____."

DAILY GOALS: DAILY FOCUS:

_____   _____
_____   _____
_____   _____
_____   _____
_____   _____
_____   _____
_____   _____
_____   _____
_____   _____

NIGHTLY SUCCESS RECAP: _____
_____
_____
_____
_____
_____
_____

NIGHTLY GRATITUDE:_____
_____
_____
_____
_____
_____
_____

DAILY FOCUS: _____

DAILY COMMITMENT: _____
_____
_____

DAILY TOP TARGET: _____
_____
_____
_____

DAILY FOCUSED MEDITATION:

"I breathe in _____, I breathe out _____."

DAILY GOALS:	**DAILY FOCUS:**
_____	_____
_____	_____
_____	_____
_____	_____
_____	_____
_____	_____
_____	_____
_____	_____
_____	_____

NIGHTLY SUCCESS RECAP: _____
_____
_____
_____
_____
_____

NIGHTLY GRATITUDE: _____
_____
_____
_____
_____
_____

ॐ

A Friendly Reminder...

Have You Ordered Your Journal For Next Year?

We Want To See Your Days Continue To Be

Full Of Gratitude, Positivity, And Success

Order Yours Today!

Step 1: Search Online - Seat Of Your Soul Daily Journal

Step 2: Order Your Journals (they also make great gifts)

Step 3: Please Leave An Online Review ☺

If you have any questions, suggestions, or feedback then please say hi.
We'd love to hear from you: mike@seatofyoursoul.com
www.SeatOfYourSoul.com

Made in the USA
Middletown, DE
27 May 2021